YOUR YOGA BUSINESS

Tools and Techniques for Success

Ava Taylor

HUMAN KINETICS

Library of Congress Cataloging-in-Publication Data

Names: Taylor, Ava, 1979- author.
Title: Your yoga business: tools and techniques for success / Ava Taylor.
Description: Champaign, IL : Human Kinetics, 2024. | Includes bibliographical references and index.
Identifiers: LCCN 2023009913 (print) | LCCN 2023009914 (ebook) | ISBN 9781718207905 (paperback) | ISBN 9781718207912 (epub) | ISBN 9781718207929 (pdf)
Subjects: LCSH: Yoga teachers--Vocational guidance. | Yoga--Economic aspects. | Entrepreneurship. | BISAC: HEALTH & FITNESS / Yoga | BUSINESS & ECONOMICS / Entrepreneurship
Classification: LCC RA781.67 .T39 2024 (print) | LCC RA781.67 (ebook) | DDC 615.8/24023--dc23/eng/20230420
LC record available at https://lccn.loc.gov/2023009913
LC ebook record available at https://lccn.loc.gov/2023009914

ISBN: 978-1-7182-0790-5 (print)

Senior Acquisitions Editor: Michelle Earle; **Developmental Editor:** Laura Pulliam; **Managing Editor:** Shawn Donnelly; **Copyeditor:** Annette Pierce; **Indexer:** Beth Nauman-Montana; **Permissions Manager:** Laurel Mitchell; **Graphic Designer:** Dawn Sills; **Cover Designer:** Keri Evans; **Cover Design Specialist:** Susan Rothermel Allen; **Photograph (cover):** © Francesca Magnani; **Photographs (interior):** © Francesca Magnani, unless otherwise noted; **Photo Asset Manager:** Laura Fitch; **Photo Production Manager:** Jason Allen; **Printer:** Walsworth

Human Kinetics books are available at special discounts for bulk purchase. Special editions or book excerpts can also be created to specification. For details, contact the Special Sales Manager at Human Kinetics.

Printed in the United States of America 10 9 8 7 6 5 4 3 2 1

The paper in this book was manufactured using responsible forestry methods.

Human Kinetics
1607 N. Market Street
Champaign, IL 61820
USA

United States and International
Website: **US.HumanKinetics.com**
Email: info@hkusa.com
Phone: 1-800-747-4457

Canada
Website: **Canada.HumanKinetics.com**
Email: info@hkcanada.com

E8372

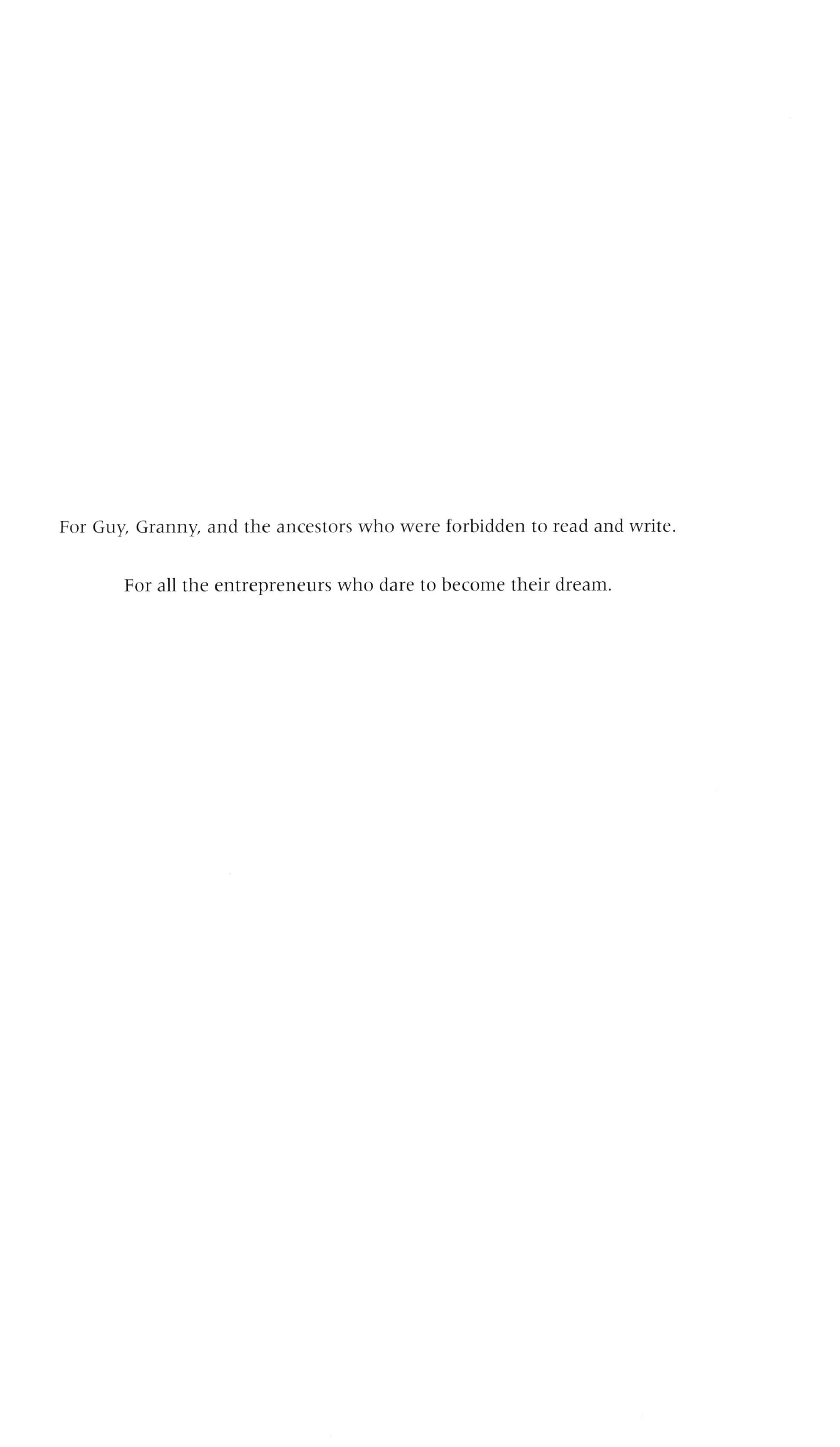

For Guy, Granny, and the ancestors who were forbidden to read and write.

For all the entrepreneurs who dare to become their dream.

CONTENTS

ACCESSING THE ONLINE CONTENT

Your Yoga Business comes with online content that is available to you for free upon purchase of a new print book or an ebook.

The HK*Propel* online content offers blank versions of all forms and worksheets in this book and the Your Yoga Business Homework activities. We are certain you will enjoy this unique online component.

Follow these steps to access the HK*Propel* online content. If you need help at any point in the process, you can contact us via email at HKPropelCustSer@hkusa.com.

If it's your first time using HK*Propel*:

1. Visit HKPropel.HumanKinetics.com.
2. Click the "New user? Register here" link on the opening screen.
3. Follow the onscreen prompts to create your HK*Propel* account.
4. Enter the access code exactly as shown below, including hyphens. You will not need to re-enter this access code on subsequent visits.
5. After your first visit, simply log in to HKPropel.HumanKinetics.com to access your digital product.

If you already have an HK*Propel* account:

1. Visit HKPropel.HumanKinetics.com and log in with your username (email address) and password.
2. Once you are logged in, navigate to Account in the top right corner.
3. Under "Add Access Code" enter the access code exactly as shown below, including hyphens.
4. Once your code is redeemed, navigate to your Library on the Dashboard to access your digital content.

Access code: TAYLOR-D9KD-LTMA-K466

Once you have signed in to HK*Propel* and redeemed the access code, navigate to your Library to access your digital content. Your license to this digital product will expire 7 years after the date you redeem the access code. You can check the expiration dates of all your HK*Propel* products at any time in My Account.

For technical support, contact us via email at HKPropelCustSer@hkusa.com. **Helpful tip:** You may reset your password from the login screen at any time if you forget it.

FOREWORD

Ava Taylor is a conductor.

No, not like the men in fancy caps managing trains in old movies. Rather, she *conducts*. She conducts as electricity causes a simple wire to glow, and she illuminates our lives with light. Ava turns the lights on, and she keeps them on, for those of us who have had the opportunity to connect with her and to share our creations with the world because of her.

I first met Ava in Soho, in the very heart of New York City—appropriate for someone who would become so pivotal to all that I love and who would become a lifelong friend. Back in the day, it was just me, a solo yoga teacher scraping together a living in the crackling, wild city. (I'd always dreamed of conquering the big city as a lonely girl who felt limited and small in the American Midwest.) I'd managed to start a yoga studio, The Fierce Club, on Elizabeth Street, just south of Houston (pro tip from a local: It's pronounced *How-stun*). It was an achingly cool space with horrifically high rent and with every class packed full of misfits and mats—and I loved it.

One afternoon, I'd agreed to host a pop-up store from a major wellness clothing brand. Class had just ended, and I walked out into the front space—I was a sweaty, happy mess—and ran straight into one of the most gorgeous, glowing humans I'd ever seen. Enter Ava Taylor.

After taking my classes a few times, she invited me to lunch. We settled into a funky booth at a café that would later become one of our regular meeting spots, and she got right to it. Ava leaned across the table and said, "Sadie, you have a gift, and I'd like to help you reach the world with it—and get paid well for doing so."

This was a shocking but strangely inviting concept for someone who'd had the belief hammered into them that wellness work should be done entirely for free if possible, but I'd struggled with that mindset. After all, my landlord didn't take good karma as rent payment.

I was intrigued: Could I both serve others and have financial abundance too?

She continued to explain that she was starting a wellness management company called YAMA Talent. She explained how she envisioned the process, with her managing the millions of details of crafting my yoga empire, so I could focus on doing what I do best: teaching and sharing my authentic self. She laid out the plan for this expansion and emphasized that I would be instrumental in helping her craft and refine the next years of my life.

Now, remember, at that time, there were very few brand deals for yogis, far fewer conferences and events we could tour, and very little awareness of our potential in the marketplace. But, as I said, Ava conducts. She took an electric possibility swirling in the ether, brought it down to earth, and showed me the light.

At the end of her pitch, she asked me what I thought about becoming one of her first clients and of jumping out into the unknown together. I said, "You had me at *hello*."

Her first act of management was to contact a multinational company who'd asked me to teach in one of their New York City stores for a day and explain to them that my email response that had asked for $120 was missing an extra zero at the end.

They gladly paid the $1,200 fee and, for the first time in my life, the exhaustion that came after such an intensive job of giving was counterbalanced by the incoming energy of proper financial compensation. The lights turned on.

Now, after I've toured the world; produced many DVDs, books, and online courses; and am able to do what I do on such a grand level because Ava took a chance on me, I can't wait for you to read the distillation of her wisdom and guidance she's offering here so generously.

It will absolutely change your mindset, spark incredible inspiration (both personally and professionally), fast-track you onto your perfect path ahead, and illuminate your journey every step of the way.

After all, that's what she does. And, in my opinion, she does it better than anyone.

Enjoy the ride,
Sadie Nardini

ACKNOWLEDGMENTS

For M, who brought me back to life.

For Granny, whose spirit lives through me, a champion for my education and using my gifts.

For my father, who, when I was three years old, said he knew I would be an author.

For my mom, who questioned why on earth I would say yes to writing a book when I already had so much on my plate.

For my friends who reminded me what an honor it is to be published and reminded me that I am worthy of being published—even when I was ready to throw in the towel.

To Michelle, who was infinitely patient with me through numerous waves of the pandemic and through my personal crises: job loss, grief for my father, divorce. Pretty much everything you could think of that could go wrong did go wrong during the writing of this book. And to Laura, who asked me to step up at the very end.

To my incredible colleagues and clients who contributed to and were an active part of the 13 years of experience that is compiled into *Your Yoga Business*; what a ride it's been.

You've all given me so much. May this book be a testament to the great dreams we had that we made real and to the future that is coming.

INTRODUCTION

The truth is, being an entrepreneur ain't easy. I know firsthand because I'm an entrepreneur myself and because I, alongside my dozens of clients (all household names in the yoga space), have built businesses together from the ground up. I know exactly how hard it is to make a great living teaching yoga, and I know how many yoga teachers are not quite getting out what they are putting in. I also know exactly what it takes to build real and sustainable growth as a yoga teacher.

This is what makes *Your Yoga Business* so powerful: It's based on real-life experience earned by working with real yoga teachers, and it's full of real-world advice. It's an honest, in-your-face look at what it really takes to make it and a comprehensive collection of the tools, techniques, and templates that you need to get to your next level. This resource is intentionally not *everything* in the world there is to know about running a successful yoga business; *Your Yoga Business* is *everything that matters.*

With a focus on the essentials, we'll comprehensively cover six parts of your yoga business:

Imagine your business, *define* your goods and services, *build* your business plan, *refine* your message, *work* your plan, and *get it done.*

My approach to building and maintaining the yoga business of your dreams is based on self-inquiry, understanding your purpose, and leaning into who you are. It relies on learning what is possible for your yoga business so you can make the best decisions about what you will build. This is done by assessing your existing yoga business so you can leverage your skills and what you've already built. It also involves customization: using strategy to make the business truly yours; mastering consistent and courageous marketing; creating new opportunities for yourself; and developing the tools, techniques, and templates you need to execute—all the plans in the world are only as good as a plan you can follow. I am as committed to your success as I have been to the success of each of my clients over the years. You will begin refining and improving your yoga business on the very first page of *Your Yoga Business*. By the time you have completed the book, you will have gained the following:

- Clarity of purpose and clarity of the direction you are taking your business
- Freedom to do what you do best: Teach (by running a more efficient business)
- Improved financial stability and security
- Empowerment to show up every day as the boss of your business so you can make your dreams a reality

Throughout the book, you'll find these features that help you identify with and implement the strategies you'll read about.

- Real Talk sidebars that feature household name yoga teachers and reinforce the overall learning objectives by highlighting what they have learned through their successes as well as their epic fails.
- Tools and templates which are the same ones my clients and I use daily to run our actual yoga businesses. *Your Yoga Business* is more than just theory; it's also a playbook that you can use to run your yoga business from day one.

- Your Yoga Business Homework activities which will urge you to think critically about your business and an appendix where all of your final answers and thoughts create a road map for your business.

Your Yoga Business isn't a book you read once and leave on the shelf. It's a reference guide you reach for time and time again as you navigate the evolving path of your yoga career. Part of running a yoga business is trial and error, but that doesn't mean you have to learn everything the hard way, which is what makes *Your Yoga Business* so unique. It allows you to tap into decades of yoga business experience, making it a true fast track for your yoga business's success.

As my granny used to say, "If you knew better, you'd do better." Welcome to *Your Yoga Business*.

PART I

IMAGINE YOUR BUSINESS

1
ENVISION YOUR DREAMS

I started practicing yoga in 2002, right out of college while living in my first adult apartment. My crazy, adventurous friend Lori—you know, the one who gets you to try "weird" things for the first time—insisted that I go with her to yoga. It was at a small yoga studio called Just-In Sight above the Hollywood Walk of Fame in Los Angeles. The owner's name was Justin. He was a young California hippie type that my friend had a crush on, and he was teaching basic hatha yoga classes. I had no mat, no leggings, and no idea that this pre–Sunday brunch activity would play the leading role in the next 20 years of my life.

I was working as a cocktail waitress at night in a celebrity-packed nightclub (also above Hollywood Boulevard) and working at an advertising agency by day. I am absolutely sure that I never went to yoga without a hangover or residue of an illegal substance in my system. I really didn't get what all the fuss over yoga was about, but it was something fun to do, and I have always loved to exercise, so I kept going pretty much every Sunday. I could not have predicted in a million years that yoga would stop being weird and start being mainstream, that I would be a world-renowned yoga business coach and the owner of two yoga-based companies, or that I would ever go to class without a hangover.

A few years later when my beloved grandmother Eddie Mae passed away, I reached a clear crossroads and had to decide how I would manage the grief I carried after her passing. I would either dive deeper into the excesses of Hollywood—where you can easily be lost for a week imbibing at a director's house in the hills—or I would dive deeper into my yoga practice on my black yoga mat. I marvel that through the haze of my grief I had the clarity to see that I was at a decisive point in my life. Even more miraculous was that I chose the yoga mat. Despite the odds and my hardwiring to cope with trauma by numbing myself to the pain, I'd somehow made a discerning and positive choice for myself. In hindsight, I can see that yoga was already working in my life.

I began practicing yoga every day and quit my job at the advertising agency to start working retail for $10 an hour folding black stretchy yoga pants for a small, unheard-of Canadian clothing company with an unpronounceable name: lululemon. I took the job mostly to give myself a way to get paid while doing yoga and to keep myself safe and surrounded by the practice. I was in awe (I am still in awe) of the fact that yoga helped this LA party girl who descended from two families with long histories of substance abuse make better choices for herself.

I committed then, at that moment in 2007, to sharing yoga with the world because I knew that if it was that powerful a catalyst for *me,* then it could have the same impact on others and could help them to live better versions of their own lives. I knew then that yoga could help people to make better choices between whatever options they would face at their own crossroads—whether the crossroads were those they stood in daily (the decisions made in each moment regarding how they would show up in the world) or the grander and more profound crossroads they would reach at pivotal moments in life, such as dealing with the loss of a loved one. Yoga to me is a catalyst for better living, and this is the reason *why* I founded my yoga business, YAMA Talent.

My purpose at YAMA Talent is to be a catalyst for better living and to bring the tools of wellness to communities of all kinds. At YAMA Talent we serve our mission daily by providing guidance, tools, and infrastructure to a diverse roster of clients in the wellness space through our main services of strategic advising, booking, and artist management.

Being a catalyst for better living is the foundation of the business and is what differentiates us from other businesses in the yoga market. Being a catalyst for better living is what informs my decision-making and guides the navigation that keeps the business heading in the right direction. Being a catalyst for better living is what shapes the goods and services we sell and the way that we market them. Being a catalyst for better living is what gets me out of bed in the morning with the necessary enthusiasm and dedication to keep putting in the work required of a small-business owner (which is what we all are as yoga professionals).

Nothing will be more important to the success of your yoga business than being able to identify and articulate your purpose. A clearly articulated purpose has a profound impact on your business by allowing you to connect with and attract the right students, collaborators, and followers. A clearly articulated purpose also turns away those who are not in alignment with your business. The goal isn't to align with everyone; the goal is to align with those who share your purpose—to align with those who believe what you believe. As author Simon Sinek says, "People don't buy what you do, they buy why you do it" (2009). You've got to start with *why*. Your *why* is your purpose as a yoga professional, and identifying your *why* and your purpose as a yoga professional is where we will begin our work.

UNDERSTAND YOUR *WHY*

The question *why* is so frequently asked, so common, that many of us have asked that very question every single day since we began to speak. The question *why* is human, as we seek answers while making our way in life and trying to understand the world around us. After all, the answer to *why* gives the reason or the purpose for everything that is done. Yet often in life, we do things without asking ourselves why—such as becoming a yoga teacher.

Ava Taylor

Old-school grassroots yoga, lululemon style, with manifesto shopping tote, circa 2007.

When I teach yoga business modules in yoga teacher training programs, I find that trainees have not asked themselves *why* they are spending hundreds of hours and thousands of dollars to become a yoga teacher. When I lead coaching sessions with yoga professionals who are already in business and looking to get to the next level, many do not remember why they began or cannot articulate why they want to keep going. Yet the most successful yoga businesses are led by professionals who know why they teach and communicate it well across every aspect of their business.

Let's take lululemon, which is a great example of a company that started with *why*. In the early days, lululemon built its brand recognition on a collection of inspiring quotes, called the manifesto, that appeared on every one of its shopping bags: *Do one thing a day that scares you. Sweat once a day to regenerate your skin. That which matters most should never give way to that which matters least. Friends are more important than money.* I remember many of them to this day. Your *why* is your manifesto and, just like it was for lululemon, your *why* will be the foundation on which you will build your name.

Your Yoga Business Homework

Identify Your Purpose

The goal of this exercise is to inspire you to clarify and articulate your *why* as a yoga professional by asking you to write a powerful, passionate purpose statement. It's more than just a statement; it's a rallying cry that will inspire you and your clients for a lifetime.

Before you begin I'd love for you to watch two videos for inspiration, Simon Sinek's 2009 TEDx Talk, "Start With Why: How Great Leaders Inspire Action," which helped me understand what matters when communicating about my business and helped me to understand what an emotional connection means in your marketing. The second is Erika Napoletano's 2012 TEDx Talk, "Rethinking Unpopular," which helped me to communicate fearlessly and gave me great support in helping me lean into my truth. I understand that starting with *why* can be difficult. Even as I was writing this book and telling the story of how I discovered my *why*, I found myself afraid to tell that truth. I was fearful of what people would think if I shared what was really awaiting me on the other side of my crossroads. I am excited to introduce you to these videos and hope they inspire you as much as they inspired me.

To support the creation of your purpose statement, here is a list of questions you can consider:

- What motivates you to teach yoga?
- Why yoga? Why now? Why you?
- What pivotal moments of your life led you to commit yourself to sharing this practice?
- How do you believe that what you have experienced or learned can help others?

Your answers to these questions will inform the writing of your purpose statement. To begin, complete the following sentences:

I teach yoga because . . . ______________________________

____

____

____

____

____

I believe . . . ______________________________

____

____

____

____

____

At this point, you may have a few short paragraphs or a few lengthy pages. Our work now will be to extract the essence of your writing into two or three powerful sentences. Don't worry about it being perfect at this point; it will take time to land on just the right few words. Do your best to pull out the key bits from your writing that speak to you—that make you *feel* something. These are the words that are the heart of your business, these are the words that are the reason your business exists, and these are the words that are your purpose and your *why*.

Write your purpose statement here:

My purpose is to . . . ______________________________

____

____

____

____

____

As an example, here is my purpose statement:

I am a catalyst for better living and bring the tools of wellness to communities of all kinds. I accomplish my mission daily by providing guidance, tools, and infrastructure to a diverse roster of clients in the wellness space.

BECOME YOUR DREAM

Now that you've articulated *why* your yoga business exists, it is time to start creating the vision of what your business will become. This powerful dreaming is where the evolution of your yoga business starts to take shape.

> *A person is a product of their dreams. So make sure to dream great dreams. And then try to live your dream.*
> *Maya Angelou*

A dream is incredibly important to the act of attainment. If you cannot visualize what you wish to become, you cannot become it. Many great thought leaders speak about our ability to make our dreams into reality, and manifestation is a concept many yoga practitioners understand and believe in. In fact, one of my favorite definitions of yoga speaks of the power of the mind to create reality. In his book *Health, Healing, and Beyond: Yoga and the Living Tradition of T. Krishnamacharya* (2011), T.K.V. Desikachar writes the following:

> The mind is the primary instrument for achieving all human ends, including happiness. Yoga is both the art and the science of perfecting that instrument . . . The Yoga of Patanjali, as taught by Krishnamacharya, bases the labors and journey of the mind, upon three fundamental premises of which we will focus on the third fundamental premise: Everything changes and is subject to change through the mind's capacity to comprehend and to shape action. And yet it is precisely in this understanding of the inevitability of change that the meaning of Yoga enters our life and beckons towards happiness. This is yoga as progression into the new . . . This is the ancient meaning: 'To move from one situation to another; to understand what I have not understood; to gain that which I lack.' The movement is in itself Yoga.
>
> Like all journeys, there must be three stages: (1) The place where we begin, (2) the choosing of our destination, (3) the effort to arrive. It is not an easy journey. Difficulties, frustrations, and disappointments will arise. We are likely to falter. That is why it must be a movement of continuous effort, and gradual progression. Always, it is movement into the new, into the previously unknown and unexperienced. And it is in this progression that we undertake the most sublime of human adventures, a path of discovery toward true and abiding happiness.

Your Yoga Business will also take you through these three stages: the beginning, the destination, and the effort we put forth to get there. In short, we as yoga practitioners and yoga business owners are always becoming, and this becoming is a labor and a journey of the mind. That journey begins with a great dream.

Real Talk

"The greatest business lesson that I have learned is to believe in yourself. As cliché as that may sound, that's where it all starts. Also, not to dismiss your inspirations. If you are inspired, you are walking in your spirit's path, and that is exactly where you are supposed to be, and it's where things just click."
Fred Antwi
Publisher/founder of Sweat Equity Lifestyle Media Group

Dreaming a great dream is not a random act or something that just happens to you while you're staring out the window watching the world go by. For your purpose of clarifying the business you wish to manifest, dreaming will require intention, hard work, and discernment—much like your yoga practice. It's a lot easier to get exactly *what* you want when you know exactly *what* it is. Before you get to work envisioning your great dream, I'd love to share a few of my favorite thoughts on dreaming.

Size doesn't matter.

Referring to a dream as great is not a reference to its actual size. It is a reference to its truth and authenticity. Your great dream is the dream that lets you use your talent and gifts to their full potential and that lets you serve your purpose in its highest capacity. Your great dream is great because it is *yours*. Your great dream is great if it gives you goosebumps when you think about it becoming real. A great dream does not have to be about making the most money or having the most followers—unless that genuinely lights you up inside.

Dream for yourself.

Many of us dream dreams that belong to someone else, either people we are emulating or people who are dictating to us how to be. Many of us aspire to someone else's definition of success. Some people spend their whole lives without considering what they really want out of life or how they really want to live. It is incredibly important that your dreams are *yours*.

Dream past your current skill set.

It's totally OK to dream about doing things you aren't ready for yet. Perhaps this is leading a yoga teacher training or speaking comfortably on stage in front of thousands. Give yourself time to develop your craft and hone your skills, but don't be afraid to dream great dreams because of your perceived lack of ability at this moment.

Dream past your current resources.

It's also okay to dream about attaining things you do not currently have the resources for—perhaps a new website, an assistant, or a clothing line. Give yourself time to develop your business and increase your revenue. As your business grows, it will allow you to do more, so don't limit your great dreams by the financial limitations that you face now. In fact, dreaming now about the things you do not have the resources for will help you clarify your dreams.

Every great achievement started with a great dream. One of the things I love best about building yoga businesses is that achieving a dream yoga business isn't about finding a mythical creature that lives in a far-off imaginary land. Rather, it's dreaming a great dream with a clear vision, choosing that you want it, and then putting in the effort to get it done. How incredibly exciting is that?

My great dream with YAMA was to have an agency that represented and was connected to the best yoga talent in the world. I wanted to get dressed up every day and go to my own office. I dreamed of seeing the name YAMA Talent on the door and having a space to do yoga in the office. I dreamed of a team of inspired people who were proud to be part of the YAMA crew. I dreamed of holiday parties with the familiar faces of my longtime clients and the children that we all watched grow up together. I dreamed of visiting exotic retreats and destinations as I spent time with my clients around the world. I dreamed of watching us grow into savvy business owners with launch parties celebrating our successes and good laughs looking back at where we all began. I dreamed of studying yoga with my clients for decades. I still have my original vision and set of goals, and it's pretty amazing to look back and see just how much of my dream I have become!

Your Yoga Business Homework

Envision Your Great Dream

Ask yourself (I dare you!): What is my great dream for my yoga business? What is it that I want to manifest? What is the greatest expression of my yoga business that will best use my talents and serve my purpose? What do my future business and future self look like and feel like? Who will I be in this dream? Who will be with me in this dream? What will I do, and how will I show up every day? Use this space to begin to tell yourself the story now of what you will become. We will get specific with how to make it a reality later.

____

____

____

____

____

____

____

____

____

____

____

____

____

____

I am so excited that you have begun articulating your purpose and envisioning your dreams. This is the foundation from which your yoga business will evolve. If you keep your purpose top of mind, it will be your compass as you move forward. And choosing a truly great dream will ensure you are successful, even if you fall a bit short of your great dream. In the next chapter, we will focus on telling your story and using components of your story to create and refine your communications.

2 TELL YOUR STORY

Telling your story is important to your career as a yoga professional because it provides the opportunity for you to be clearly understood and seen in context. In this chapter, we will use your story to create a remarkable bio, a tagline, and content pillars for your business that you will use in your marketing. Your story is an account of your unique life experiences. For our purposes, the story you want to tell is of your life as it relates to your career as a yoga professional. It is an account of your choices, your actions, what happened, how you felt, and what you learned. It's an account of your hopes, dreams, fears, and motivations. It's your journey used purposefully.

Telling your story is inspiring because it is a human experience full of progress, setbacks, and learning—a story that illustrates to your followers that you are leading them skillfully on the same path that you have traveled. Your clients respond well to knowing more about who you are and where you've come from. As a teacher and as a leader who is out front inspiring others to live their best lives, what more powerful act could you perform than to share the remarkable truth of your own beginning, progress, and past?

Nothing is less inspiring than a seemingly perfect know-it-all who appears to have life all figured out. I doubt you disagree. Yet often we do not tell our stories powerfully, and leave much to be misunderstood. This is why it is important to discuss the false perception of yoga teachers alongside our discussion of storytelling. As yoga students, we often value perfection over progress and project a perceived perfection onto our teachers, who we see as radiant human beings, able to do amazing things with their bodies and who inspire us with their seemingly perfect and amazing lives. We project perfection onto these very human beings who sit before us in positions of power. We look up to them, and we emulate them. We create a false perception of who they are, how they got to where they are, and what their behavior should be.

Anyone who's gotten to know a successful yoga teacher on a personal level knows that they will tell you, oftentimes heartbreakingly, just how imperfect they really are. And the yoga teacher will tell you they never pretended to be perfect (or pretended to be anything). This may be true, but were they honest about who they really were? While we cannot fully control what others project on us, we can shape that projection and control the narrative a lot more than most yoga teachers want to take responsibility for. How you are perceived as a yoga teacher is often equal parts what is said and what isn't said. Which is why I encourage my clients to tell their own stories powerfully, honestly, and truthfully. One of the best things about telling your story truthfully is that you unlock some of the magic, mystery, and misconceptions around who you are and how you got to be where you are. There's a freedom in it for you as someone out front, and unless you really are perfect, your story of progress will be incredibly inspiring because it allows people to feel as if they can make progress too!

I'll never forget a conversation with my first client, who was a yoga teacher and lifestyle expert, Sadie Nardini, back in her early days. She had a perfect handstand and naturally bright red hair and scissored bangs and loved to wear leather and to sing classic rock. *Rock Your Yoga* was an idea (which we turned into a global brand and online yoga series) and style of teaching that were authentically hers. After every workshop she taught, we would discuss the content: what worked, what didn't, what we could do better next time. One conversation focused on her dharma talk, the opening act so to speak. It might seem odd to review a yoga class in as much detail as we did, but we wanted to create a mind-blowing experience. One day we decided to take a chance and to tell the real story of her past.

Sadie had grown up poor and unsophisticated in Iowa. She was made fun of and experienced a debilitating disease in her teens. She could barely walk, let alone do a handstand. One day, her mother gave her a yellowed copy of Richard Hittleman's *Yoga* in the hopes that it would help. Sadie literally crawled out of bed and laid on the floor attempting to mirror the postures. Because of her physical limitations, she could not replicate what she saw in the book, but even done "incorrectly," the postures made her feel better, so she kept doing them. For two years, those awkward stretches were her practice, and that was her beginning. I was there when she told the story for the first time, and the energy in the room was palpable. She connected with the students on a visceral level and gained their trust and loyalty by being vulnerable. Her confiding in them gave them confidence (many for the first time) that maybe they too could someday do a handstand—no matter where they were starting from physically. And most importantly, everyone learned that even if they never got to that picture-perfect posture, they could feel great and transform themselves just the same.

It is better to live in your own destiny imperfectly than to live an imitation of somebody else's life with perfection.

The Bhagavad Gita

I believe that everyone's story is remarkable, and that remarkability is relative. You don't need to have made heroic shifts in your life or to have overcome tragedy. Whatever your story of progress is, I assure you, it is enough to inspire your students. Our work now is to simply tell it like it is. We have a list of writing exercises that we use at YAMA to do our storytelling:

- Request testimonials and feedback.
- Write a remarkable bio.
- Create a tagline.
- Brand your weird.
- Extract your pillars.

The rest of this chapter will lead you through each of these exercises as you craft your unique, remarkable story. It will set the stage for the exciting journey through the later steps to building your yoga business.

REQUEST TESTIMONIALS AND FEEDBACK

To begin your storytelling process, we will focus on how others perceive you—rather than focusing on the stories that you tell yourself or tell others about yourself—by conducting a testimonial and feedback request. The testimonial and feedback request gives you an opportunity to observe how you are showing up in the market in relation to how you want to show up and to identify opportunities for improvement. It's so much better to know what people think than to assume it.

Don't be shy about asking for testimonials and feedback. Most students are happy to have a chance to be heard, to share their opinion, and to give you both perspective and love. The information you receive from this exercise will also help you to better align your purpose and your benefits as a teacher.

Your Yoga Business Homework

Request Testimonials and Feedback

Testimonial and feedback requests can be conducted in several ways, such as on paper after a group class or a private session, via email, via chat or direct message on social media, or even through an online survey. Make sure that your students know that their responses can be anonymous if they wish and also that you will not use them publicly without their express consent.

I suggest that you ask a mix of both new and long-standing students some of the following questions:

- What drew you to me or my class in the first place?
- If you could describe me or my classes in three words, what would they be?
- What keeps you coming back to class? Why do you stay my friend?
- What are my most positive traits?
- What do you love most about my offerings?
- What might stop you from coming back to class?
- What is one thing that you wish you knew more about me or my business?
- What is one thing you wish I did differently?
- What is your favorite memory of me?

Feel free to add more to this list of questions. Remember, now is your time to get to know what your students are thinking on a deeper level.

Available online on HK*Propel*.

The answers you receive from your testimonial and feedback requests are the beginning of a list of all the ways you can improve and add value to your students' lives. It's powerful and validating to see these testimonials—and you also have great use for them within your yoga business. These answers provide the beginning of a list of valuable potential improvements or adjustments that you could make in your business if you deem them appropriate. Remember, everyone has an opinion, and just because you are asking for feedback doesn't mean that you have to act on every piece of feedback that you receive. For most students, the ask in itself means more than the action that comes from it, although business owners are often pleasantly surprised by the creativity their students have as outsiders looking in.

The truth is, not everyone will love you or your business, and not everyone needs to. Yes, your goal is to find those for whom your work resonates and those who believe what you believe, but that does not mean you should run a business with tunnel vision, where you have no idea how you are affecting the market or where you miss out on valuable client observations.

WRITE A REMARKABLE BIO

Let's do a quick refresher of what a basic bio is before we discuss what makes a bio remarkable. (For those of you already saying to yourself that you aren't remarkable, let me remind you that *everyone* is remarkable!) Simply put, a bio is a short story about a person's life. For our purposes, your bio is a short story of your life as it relates to your career as a yoga teacher. A bio is not to be confused with a resume, although most yoga teacher bios are resumes, with great focus placed on what they've done, how many years of training they have and with whom, and a laundry list of credentials—all without details regarding why they took those actions or the amazing lessons they learned along the way.

A remarkable bio combines your resume and your *lifeline*. A lifeline is a timeline of pivotal moments—those that led you to teach, those that illustrate the impact yoga has had on your life, those that speak to your greatest successes and failures. A remarkable bio is one that tells your true story, not the edited version you think a yoga teacher should tell. Your true story allows your audience to feel that you have shared life experiences that form a powerful and lasting bond, something that is vital to success in an intimate service-based business such as teaching yoga. A remarkable bio is important to your yoga business because it allows you to connect with your audience and to establish trust and credibility.

As you prepare to write your remarkable bio, beware of a common yoga pitfall. Many yogis have a hard time writing their bio because they are afraid of disappointing their students or peers. The potential for disappointment comes from them having not been transparent about who they are or where they came from in the first place. If you are busy being the kind of yoga teacher you think you're supposed to be rather than the one you really are, writing a remarkable bio can be tricky. It's like taking off your costume. Your transition to truthfulness may cause some client turnover in the beginning, but the overall result will be a loyal community and a sense of freedom for you as teacher and business owner to let your practice and business be yours. There's a big difference between sharing the truth about the progress you have made in your life and what my granny called "airing your dirty laundry." You can tell your story powerfully, but leave out the gory details.

Speaking of progress, sometimes as teachers—who have come such a long way and done so much work—we forget the value in the story of our own progress, the things we have learned along the way, the moments that have shaped us, our battle scars, and our battle cries. Do not doubt that your growth and your achievements are important to others who are around you.

Your Yoga Business Homework
Craft a Lifeline and Write Your Remarkable Bio

To begin writing your remarkable bio, start by crafting a lifeline—a timeline of important events in your life that have shaped who you are and the things that you are passionate about. Your lifeline will include the pivotal moments that have led you to become a yoga teacher, that have built your family, and that have shaped your *why*. Write or record your pivotal moments and also what you thought and what lessons you learned at each of those pivotal moments.

For example, some pivotal moments of my story, which you have already read about, include taking my first yoga class in Hollywood, California, in 2002, my grandmother passing away in 2007, and my starting YAMA Talent in 2009. When I take those same pivotal moments and address them as part of a lifeline, they develop into this:

- I took my first yoga class in Hollywood, California, in 2002 *even though I thought yoga was weird.*
- My grandmother passed away in 2007, *and I made a choice for myself to use yoga for healing my grief rather than numbing myself with substances. I made the decision to commit myself to sharing the practice of yoga with the world.*
- I started YAMA Talent in 2009 *and took the insane plunge into entrepreneurship. Did I know what I was doing? No, but did I believe I could figure it out along the way? Yes!*

As you can see, the details added in the lifeline give depth, insight, and understanding of my experience by including useful and colorful details that enhance my story. With this new, remarkable material, write or rewrite your bio to include more of your story. Be honest, vulnerable, and transparent and have fun! This is where the true power of your remarkability lies. Your remarkable bio once edited should total approximately 300 words. I also find it useful to create shorter edits of 200 and 100 words each.

____

____

____

____

____

CREATE A TAGLINE

Now that you have crafted a remarkable bio, let's keep going with your powerful storytelling by developing a tagline. A powerful tagline is also known as a catchphrase or a slogan, and extracting one from within your storytelling is a great way to establish market-friendly consistency for your yoga business.

As an example, we found Sadie's tagline by creating a list of our favorite Sadie-isms she said in class and putting them up on a white board. We chose the one we liked best: Rock Your Yoga. (We eventually developed the tagline into a full-blown business: classes, workshops, a TV show, and book titled *Rock Your Yoga,* a Rockstar

Yoga Teacher Training, and more.) A small piece of messaging can be used powerfully to shape and strengthen a yoga business.

Your Yoga Business Homework

Create a Great Tagline

Make a list of some of your favorite sayings; these may be key words or phrases, the punch line of your favorite jokes, sutras, quotes, or inspirations. You know, the ones that you end up saying to your clients all the time. Chances are, if it works in the classroom or in a private session, it is likely it will work on your website, on hard copy collateral, as the title of an event, or as a hashtag, too!

___

___

___

___

BRAND YOUR WEIRD

The best branding is to be more you.

One of my favorite techniques to further develop and enhance a business's storytelling is called *brand your weird*. Branding your weird is important because it helps to differentiate you in the market. I often field questions from teachers who feel they will never be able to stand out in the market, to which I reply: Brand your weird. If you feel like just another yoga teacher, it's because you aren't telling your story with enough detail or are not articulating what makes you unique. Just as each and every yoga teacher has a remarkable story to tell, so is each yoga teacher unique and weird! Even those of you who think you are tragically normal can brand your weird. So what does it mean to be unique as a yoga teacher? Let's take a closer look.

Teach Like Yourself

Even if you follow a strict lineage, are part of a larger teaching organization or school, or teach a set sequence, you can still make it *yours*, as all the most successful yoga teachers eventually do. You can think about *brand your weird* as your style, your unique interpretation of yoga. I often think of yoga as music, and teachers as musicians—all musicians emulate in the beginning, but eventually, over time, their unique style will develop. As Miles Davis, the famous jazz trumpeter, bandleader, and composer, said, "Sometimes you have to play a long time to be able to play like yourself."

Real Talk

"The point is that you have to be you and see who surrounds you."
Sadie Nardini
E-RYT 500 and online wellness entrepreneur

Your Yoga Business Homework

Identify and Brand Your Weird

To begin identifying and articulating your weird, ask yourself the following questions and use the space to write: What sets you apart from other yoga teachers and yoga businesses? How is your interpretation of yoga like no one else's?

____

____

____

____

EXTRACT YOUR PILLARS

The next step in articulating your business is called extracting your pillars. A pillar in its most common use is a vertical support that strengthens a structure, such as a house. Using this definition for our purposes, the house is your business, and the pillars are the key conversations that hold your business up—the conversations so essential to your overall business and what it stands for that they support your business. When you described your lifeline as part of your story, you articulated important events in your life that have shaped who you are, things that you are

Albania Salas (left), Oneika Mays (right), and me during the COVID-19 pandemic. The worst of times brought out the best of YAMA Talent: being resilient, supporting each other in community, and showing up for our yoga businesses.

passionate about, and vital lessons that you have learned along the way. Within these events, passions, and learnings, you will find the pillars of your brand.

For example, some of the pillars of YAMA are empowerment, opportunity, clarity of purpose and direction, and practice. These are the key conversations that comprise all of my work at YAMA, and every product or service that I create aligns with one of my pillars. My pillars *are* my business; they are the "contents of my content," and it is my goal to bring them to life through my branding and service models.

I bring the empowerment pillar to life through the educational tools that we have created, such as The Catalyst online business school for yogis and the reBUILD online video series, which was created specifically as a response to COVID-19. Because empowerment is a pillar of our company, we have a "done *with* you" approach, rather than a "done *for* you" approach. Our goal is to teach yoga teachers to be great small-business owners, and in addition to our online products, we support them through free content on our website, workshops that I teach, and more.

I also bring opportunity to life through our educational tools and through a strategic advising and consulting process called pitching, where we work with teachers on increasing their opportunities by helping them create great pitch materials and then making the connections on their behalf. I also pride myself on being a free "plug" for the community and doing my best whenever possible to connect the right teachers to the right opportunities no matter what our professional relationship might be.

The clarity of purpose and direction pillar lives predominantly in a consulting process called the *road map*, where we work with a yoga teacher to assess their existing business and help them to create a business plan. I conduct road maps one-on-one. This is a mainstay of the work that YAMA does, and you are working through a robust version of the road map process in this book.

I bring practice to life by maintaining my personal practice as a yoga student and taking classes at studios around the world, both in person and online to continue studying the practice of yoga. I will never forget someone on the phone asking me, "Do you even *do* yoga?" I laughed and said, "Yes. Yes I do." It's an important part of YAMA's branding that we consistently practice yoga.

Your Yoga Business Homework

Extract Your Pillars

Let's take time to list three pillars—the essential conversations that your business consists of. Here's a suggestion to help you get started: For most yoga businesses, yoga itself is a pillar.

1. ______________________

2. ______________________

3. ______________________

All of the written storytelling you have completed in this chapter will be used to customize the goods and services you offer and used in the components of your marketing. Great work thus far! Up next, we will work on how to visually tell your story!

3
CRAFT YOUR VISUAL IDENTITY

Courtesy of Finlay Wilson.

An on-brand photo of the Kilted Yogi, Finlay Wilson, in the Scottish Highlands.

One of my favorite stories that illustrates the value of visual branding is that of my long-term client and also oh-so-fabulous friend, Finlay Wilson. Finlay is a truly one-of-a-kind teacher, artist, and creator. He is super committed to the benefits of the practice, and he is super Scottish. Finlay became an Internet sensation in 2016 when he did yoga in his kilt in the rugged Scottish Highlands and cheekily answered the big question, "What's under the kilt?" It was a raging success.

I handled the negotiations for the Kilted Yoga brand and its sequel, WILD Kilted Yoga, and eventually supported the expansion of the brand into a website, marketing materials, merchandise, calendars, live TV segments, and more. The business has branched into many avenues and will continue to do so, but there is always a unifying factor across the various elements of the Kilted Yoga brand: the tartan and the kilt. In the same way that "kilts are a piece of heritage that reaches from the past to the present" (Wilson 2019, 19), for the Kilted Yoga brand, the tartan and the kilt are (pardon the pun) the thread that weaves Finlay's yoga business together. Kilted Yoga is a great example of a brand with a strong visual identity because it's so easy to see the consistency. You do not need something as obvious as tartan or a kilt to weave your visual brand together well. Every yoga business can have a strong visual identity.

One of the issues with building a strong visual identity is that we don't often look at all of our points of contact at once. I like to call this comprehensive look the view of your brand from 30,000 feet (the cruising altitude of an airplane which lets you see a vast landscape at once). While we are busy running our businesses, we tend to look at one visual element at a time. We will create a postcard when we need one, we will refresh a page on our website, or we will quickly rush to create a new social media account, but rarely do we look at all of the points of contact at once and ask ourselves, "Is my visual identity cohesive? Is my visual identity as strong as it could be? Is my visual identity threading my brand together?"

Getting to the next level requires increasing your opportunities and revenue, and to do so requires more brand recognition (people hearing about and seeing your business and remembering it!). This is why it is important that your visual identity be consistent and complete. A strong visual identity increases the memorability of your yoga business because there are recognizable visual elements at each point of contact. Many clients who come to me to elevate their business to the next level are seeking marketing or strategic support, and I often have to insist that we start our work together with a thorough brand refresh that improves their visual identity. You'd be surprised how many yoga businesses haven't ever considered their visual identity, let alone done so comprehensively, or that have dysfunctional points of contact, such as a webpage with a broken link; a simple miss like that costs your business greatly. Every opportunity to obtain and retain a client is important, which is why you always want to put your best foot forward. A strong visual identity will let your business work for you.

In chapter 10, we will take a comprehensive look at your current business's visual identity from 30,000 feet. Right now, in this chapter, however, I want you to imagine and envision the visual identity of your dreams.

COMPONENTS OF VISUAL IDENTITY

A visual identify is made up of several characteristics: purpose, pillars, personality, color, font type and size, and key imagery. Let's take a look at each of these in more detail.

Purpose

Simplicity is often underrated. Your visual identity doesn't need to be complicated, high tech, or expensive to be well done.

In chapter 1, you identified your purpose as a yoga business professional, focusing on a written text-based way to communicate why your business exists. Now, I ask you to consider a visual way to communicate why your business exists. In what ways can you visually communicate your purpose? Are there particular colors or key images you can use to bring your *why* to life? For example, if community is a pillar of your business, you may use key images of groups of people practicing, eating, talking, or walking together.

Pillars

In chapter 2, we clarified the pillars of your business, and it's vital that the pillars of your business be visible! A strong visual presence for your pillars usually relates to the structural organization of your visual identity. Is there a proper home for each pillar on all of your points of contact? For example, if nutrition is a pillar of your brand, then the word *nutrition* should be visually present on your website, on your social media bios, and so on.

Personality

As we established earlier, you are your yoga business. Yet so many of us do not let our personalities shine when it comes to our visual branding. Does your visual identity look and feel like you? If not, how could it look and feel more like you? If someone who knew you personally looked at your visual branding, would they say it looks and feels like you? Or would there be a disconnect from who you are and how you are presenting your yoga business? I love to encourage teachers to consider using visual representations of people, places, and things that inspire them as part of their visual brand. For instance, if music is a huge component of your business personality, why not have imagery of your favorite musicians? Or, if mystical poetry is a component of your business personality, why not have a montage or collage of poetry as a visual element? Visual representations of your inspirations can add a nice layer of texture to your overall visual identity.

Real Talk

"It's absurd to compare me to another person. I'm unique and they're unique. . . . You can't compare yourself with someone else."
Bryan Kest
Yoga practitioner, teacher, and creator of Power Yoga

Color

Because colors have meaning and convey emotion, visual branding uses color in a way similar to how they are attributed to the chakras. Your color palette sets the tone for your visual branding. Refer to the Colors and Their Associated Meanings sidebar to see what colors mean and emote in a marketing sense. A common mistake with color is trying to use too many; this creates confusion because there are so many meanings and emotions being conveyed at once.

Font Type and Size

The type and size of font you choose also convey meaning. This may seem like a minor element of visual identity, but you can completely revamp your business just by changing the font. Oftentimes, the font is an afterthought rather than an intentional method to communicate, which weakens the visual identity; you'll see a playful, bubbly, childlike font used to communicate and sell a serious product. This mismatched visual identity will still work, but if it were aligned, it would work much better.

Key Imagery

Key images are cornerstone images or elements of images that form the main point of your visual message. It's important to choose key imagery that is powerful and illustrative of either you, your purpose, your personality, emotion, or a product that is a core part of your business. Many yoga businesses use key imagery that is not significant or related to their business's identity, such as stock art, or overusing a logo, which might mean something to you but doesn't necessarily mean anything to your clients. Poor choices for key imagery waste a lot of the prime real estate of your visual brand. Many yoga businesses also omit key imagery that *is* significant to their business, such as an image of themselves. After all, you are your yoga business.

When it comes to your visual identity, keep it simple; make it clean, make it clear, and make it consistent.

Colors and Their Associated Meanings

- *Red*—creates a sense of urgency and encourages appetite (so it's frequently used by fast-food chains). It physically stimulates the body and is associated with movement, excitement, and passion.
- *Blue*—associated with peace, water, and reliability. Blue provides a sense of security, curbs appetite, and stimulates productivity. It's the most common color used by conservative brands looking to promote trust in their products.
- *Green*—associated with health, power, and nature. It is often used to promote environmental issues. Green stimulates harmony in the brain and encourages balance, leading to decisiveness.
- *Purple*—commonly associated with royalty, wisdom, and respect. It stimulates problem-solving as well as creativity. It is frequently used to promote beauty and antiaging products.
- *Orange and yellow*—cheerful colors that promote optimism. They are often used to draw in impulsive buyers and window shoppers.
- *Black*—associated with authority, stability, and strength. It is often a symbol of intelligence, but it can become overwhelming if used too frequently.
- *Gray*—symbolizes feelings of practicality and solidarity. Too much gray can lead to feelings of "nothingness" and depression.
- *White*—associated with purity, cleanliness, and safety. It can be used to project an absence of color or neutrality. White space helps spark creativity because it can be perceived as an unaltered, clean slate.

ADDITIONAL CONSIDERATIONS RELATED TO VISUAL IDENTITY

Your yoga business strategy activity for this chapter is to create a visual cues mood board, which will become your visual guide as you build the business of your dreams. But before we create this, I want to share a few important things to think about regarding visual identity:

- *Beware of catfishing.* Whether you intentionally deceive your clients or not, a yoga business with poor visual branding can confuse or mislead your clients. For example, if you are a strict, disciplined-style yoga teacher and your visual identity features candy colors and meme-style quotes, your clients may feel that you are not who you portray yourself to be. You can take a look at the websites of some of your favorite teachers as a quick way to observe this accidental catfishing. How many of the websites would you look at and think, this website doesn't reflect who they actually are?
- *Be you!* Many yoga businesses play "looky see, looky do" when it comes to visual branding—and end up looking more like each other than like themselves. I love to draw inspiration from all disciplines: art, music, fashion, food, sports, corporations, you name it. Start paying attention to the visual identities of some of the brands you love and the personalities you follow, and you will begin to notice the characteristics of their unique visual identity. Don't be afraid to have a visual brand that doesn't seem "yogic." The entire concept of what a

yoga business is or looks like is completely outdated. As one of my favorite teachers used to say, "There are as many yogas as there are yous." Your visual branding can be as unique as you are.

- *To logo or not to logo?* I believe that a logo is a "nice to have but not need to have" element of your brand. Many well-known yoga businesses use a brand name or tagline consistently but not necessarily a logo (i.e., a shape or form that represents them when they are not present). Because you are the yoga business, it isn't as important to have a symbol that represents you—you can represent you. I find that the use of a logo can be problematic for a lot of yoga businesses. I have seen yoga business owners get stuck for months trying to come up with a genius logo, and when they do, they then assume that the public knows what the logo stands for (thereby not taking the time to explain it thoroughly). What they end up with is branding that might look cool but doesn't say much about their actual business or doesn't mean much to the public.

Your Yoga Business Homework

Imagine Your Visual Identity

To help you create a visual representation of the visual identity of your dream brand, create a mood board by compiling on a poster board visual cues for the following characteristics: color, key imagery, font type and size, purpose, pillars, personality, and emotion. These should represent the ideal visual identity of your yoga business. Once you have built a board that looks and feels like you, share the board with a colleague or a student for their feedback. In chapter 10, you'll have a chance to assess how your existing brand's visual identity matches up against the visual identity of your dreams.

© YAMA Talent

Available online on HK*Propel*.

Understanding the importance of a strong visual identity and creating the visual identity of your dream business are foundational concepts to use to take your business to the next level. We will now move on from what your business looks like to what business types and service models your business is made of. Before you can paint the house, you've got to build it!

PART II

DEFINE YOUR GOODS AND SERVICES

4
EXPLORE BUSINESS TYPES

It took me a few years of gathering data through my real-life experience working with hundreds of yoga teachers—each with different opportunities and goals at different stages of their careers—to learn that there were separate and distinct service models that each of these yoga teachers created their business from. With time, I could see how a yoga teacher in a big city such as New York or Los Angeles was making their living and how a yoga teacher who lived in a rural environment was making theirs. With time, I could see how a yoga teacher who had star quality or prior acting experience would be drawn toward certain opportunities and how someone with prior corporate experience might be drawn toward teaching yoga in a corporate setting. No matter the type of yoga teacher or the kind of yoga business that they had built for themselves, it became quite clear that there were several types of business models and that they were made of different types of services.

It was an exciting moment in the development of YAMA when I was able to codify the business types and service models because it helped us all understand and make sense of the larger professional yoga landscape and gave me a framework to support the development of my clients. The business types and service models are not set in stone, and as the industry continues to evolve, I expect to see the business types and services models continue to expand as the industry does.

Many yoga professionals move between business types and service models during different phases of their careers.

Also, each yoga teacher comprises a unique type of yoga business and uses each service model differently, meaning they will not totally fit into any one business type or service model, and many yoga professionals move between these business types and service models during different phases of their careers. Understanding the business types and service models helps yoga professionals to understand the breadth of the opportunities available in order to construct the business of their dreams.

BUSINESS TYPES

There are several yoga business types—hobby, career, hometown hero, regional rock star, household name, and online only. Let's take a closer look at the characteristics and pros and cons of each.

Hobby

A hobby yoga teacher is someone who teaches part time and has another job or main source of income. This is also lovingly known as a yoga side hustle. One of the best things about being a hobby teacher is that it takes a lot of pressure off of your yoga business because you don't need to make your entire livelihood from teaching yoga—a true silver lining. I can't tell you how many people fall in love with yoga, start teaching, and then fall out of love the minute they need it to be their sole source of income. I often tell people, "Don't quit your day job" because there's nothing wrong with having full-time employment and serving as a yoga teacher on the side. Being a hobby teacher is no less professional or important than any of the other business types. A hobby career can be built out just as thoughtfully and thoroughly as a full-time teaching career. Another bonus of the hobby business type is that it allows for more efficient use of your time. When teaching yoga is your second job, the time you spend on it is limited because of your other obligations, and therefore must be potent and effective. It seems counterintuitive that having limited time to work with can create better results when compared to unlimited time, but that is exactly the case.

Real Talk

"Business is one of the most creative places in the world."
Cyndi Lee
Teacher of mindful yoga and author

Career

The career business type is a yoga teacher who makes their full income teaching yoga. This is also known as the main hustle. Career teachers are full-time teachers whose entire livelihood comes from their yoga business. This is a great goal that many who enter the field of teaching aspire to. It usually takes six to eight years to become a full-time teacher, so I always encourage folks to think about a reasonable and realistic amount of time to transition from being a hobby yoga teacher to a career yoga teacher. I have also experienced many instances in which the employer you have while you are a hobby teacher is happy to share in your goals and growth and to be part of your professional transition by offering reduced hours and less responsibility while you ramp up your yoga business.

Hometown Hero

A hometown hero is a career yoga teacher who is well known in the city that they live in—a big fish in a small pond! Many yoga teachers I work with have built extremely successful and lucrative careers without ever leaving their hometown. The decision to be a hometown hero is often based on personal considerations that allow you to build a robust and financially rewarding career while still being able to sleep in your own bed or tuck your kids in every night. Most teachers who move on to become a regional rock star or household name have become heroes in their hometowns first. I have found it rare that anyone becomes a regional rock star or a household name without having become a hometown hero first.

Regional Rock Star

A regional rock star is a career yoga teacher who is well known in the region within a two- to three-hour radius from their hometown. This is a manageable distance that allows them to get away and cultivate other communities while still allowing them to have a strong, consistent presence in their hometown as a base. Oftentimes folks who become regional rock stars own a yoga studio or a business that they need to nurture or spend significant time in, which makes certain elements of touring and traveling less feasible—touring and traveling being key steps to becoming a household name. For example, traveling out of town regularly (once or twice a month) and maintaining a healthy hometown presence is difficult. It can be done, but it is difficult. When Sadie Nardini was a regional rock star, she also owned a yoga studio. We could see quite clearly that in order to become a household name she would no longer be able to run the studio, so we created a plan for her to get out of her ownership share of the studio so she could pursue her goal of becoming a household name.

Household Name

The household name business type is a yoga teacher who is well known on the national or international stage—who we in the industry would consider a celebrity with true household name recognition. These teachers have huge followings both in person and online and travel extensively in order to maintain momentum and relationships with their communities. This is the rarest career type for a yoga teacher and requires an all-in time commitment. Many of my clients who are household name yoga teachers never unpack their suitcases and have had to adjust their personal lives to fit the reality of touring and traveling in order to maintain this level of recognition. Surprisingly, the household name business type does not necessarily produce the highest financial earnings. In the yoga world, fame and fortune do not always go hand in hand.

Real Talk

"Over 25 years of flying all over the world has gotten old. COVID gave me a little break, and I don't know if I want to go back. So, how do I continue to get my teachings out there? I've been going into a filming studio and doing high-quality video courses for learning management systems, with some of them translated into different languages. So I'm actually looking at my retirement and looking at what will be a business model that will keep some money coming in and keep my teachings out there."
Anodea Judith
Author, public speaker, and therapist

Online Only

In our modern day and age, some yoga teachers instruct solely online and have very little interaction with their students in real life. Conversely, some yoga students have never practiced in an actual yoga studio. I once met a yoga teacher trainee who shared that when she walked into the studio to begin yoga teacher training, it was the first time she had ever been in an actual yoga classroom. I was floored.

The online-only business model is unique and entrepreneurial—pretty much anything goes, and it has its own set of pros and cons. You don't need to look much further than yoga YouTube channels or Instagram influencers with tons of subscribers to see examples of yoga teachers who have excelled in an online-only capacity. This doesn't mean that they don't eventually broaden their business to incorporate some of the other service models, but their priority was and is the online space. The Internet is vast, and I do not believe that it has been fully conquered in any way. However, when setting out to build an online-only business, you must recognize the length of time and the kind of content commitment that will be required in order to gain traction and to make it a successful service model. You cannot just wake up, snap your fingers, and become Yoga With Adriene or Koya Webb, for example. In 2014, I founded and launched a multichannel YouTube network called the Digital Yoga Network and have watched the development of the online-only space closely for many years. I have seen firsthand the time and investment it takes to develop an online-only business.

What I find more reasonable for most yoga teachers is to use the online space strategically within their larger yoga business rather than having it as their only business type. It's much more realistic and can still be incredibly potent and profitable.

Your Yoga Business Homework

Consider the Business Types

Take a moment here to consider the different business types and answer these questions:

Which of the business types resonates most with you and why? What other questions do you have about this business type? ____________________

____

____

Which of the business types resonates least with you and why? ____________________

____

____

Which of the business types did you find most surprising when you learned more about them and why? ____________________

____

____

Which business type does your favorite teacher use? ____________________

____

____

YOGA SERVICE MODELS

Now that we have established the types of yoga businesses that exist, let's take a look at the service models they are made of. Service models are the building blocks of your yoga business—the literal goods and services that you offer. A good is a tangible product that you sell, and a service is a nontangible product or task that you sell. Your yoga goods and services are what your clients consume and spend money on within your business.

Understanding the variety of opportunities available to you as you build your business is important because it allows you to more easily envision and construct the yoga business of your dreams. Keep in mind that all of these goods and services can be offered in person and online.

Service models are the building blocks of your yoga business—the literal goods and services that you offer.

In the yoga business there is a standard set of yoga service models: one-to-ones, group sessions, conferences or festivals, workshops, immersions, trainings, and retreats. We will cover how you package and sell your goods and services in chapter 8. First, let's take a closer look at the characteristics and the pros and cons of each service model. You will also think about your current business and what service models you might want to develop.

One-to-One Sessions

One-to-one sessions involve one student and one teacher. In this type of service, you teach a single student. There are endless types of one-to-one services: yoga privates, business coaching, mentoring, and nutrition sessions. When properly weighted within your yoga business, one-to-one sessions ought to be the highest valuation of your time because you serve a single student, and this model creates the most intimate business relationship. We will dive deep into how to cultivate, maintain, and level up a successful one-to-one business in chapter 5.

Group Sessions

Group sessions, which include classes and lectures, are short-duration (up to 90 minutes) offerings that are available at a reasonable price. Examples might include a yoga class or lecture on root chakra flow. Think of this service model as your first date with the market because it requires a low commitment of time and money for someone to get to know you.

Conferences or Festivals

The conference or festival service model consists of yoga offerings that vary in duration and price and are typically hosted by an outside organization—although you can absolutely create your own conference or festival, which is an entire service model of its own! Conferences and festivals provide access to large groups of students at once, and usually those students are folks that you would not normally have access to. While these engagements in and of themselves usually are not lucrative, these events provide a good opportunity for exposure to your yoga business. I recommend seeking out these kinds of appearances after you have developed the other service models for your business to allow the exposure to work for you. It doesn't make

YAMA Talent coproduced the group yoga session during the Obama administration's annual White House Easter Egg Roll.

sense to get in front of a lot of students if you have not developed proper goods and services that you can offer them. I like to think of the conference and festival service model as your speed date with the market.

Workshops

The workshop service model consists of events lasting 90 minutes to three hours that require a larger time commitment from students and are often sold at a higher price than individual classes and lectures. These events are an opportunity to dive deeper into your pillars of content. I encourage you to think about your own pillars and how you can further bring to life what is important to your business when you have more time to spend with your students. For example, a workshop on understanding the root chakra will give you an opportunity to share your extensive knowledge of the root chakra, or perhaps you could hold a root chakra flow yoga class and lecture combined.

Immersions

The immersion service model consists of more than three hours of programming offered in a half or full day, full weekend, or multiday format. These are higher-priced programs that require more investment from your students and also more time in preparation and delivery from you. A healthy, well-rounded yoga business will regularly offer some type of higher-commitment program, and these are great ways to increase revenue outside of training teachers. An example of an immersion could be a weeklong chakra immersion that explores all seven chakras, with each chakra having its own workshop (class and lecture) each day.

Products and Merchandise

In addition to yoga programs as a service model, you can create and sell products and merchandise within your yoga business. It doesn't matter how long you have been teaching or how big a following you have.

Products

The product service model consists of opportunities to partner with and create goods that match your brand characteristics, helping to diversify your business and amplify your brand recognition. Products are an opportunity to create revenue and interaction within your yoga business by creating additional ways for your students to buy and buy into your brand. For example, you might sell essential oils that align with each chakra. I like to think of products as a way to keep an existing relationship fresh.

Merchandise

The merchandise service model consists of signature ID products that match your brand characteristics and feature your brand name, logo, or likeness. Industries such as art, music, fashion, food, sports, and corporations know how important it is to leverage the merchandise service model within a business. I have even heard touring agents say that "the tour is only as good as the merch table." This is especially true in our current age of showing folks what we believe in. Like the lululemon manifesto story I shared in chapter 1, well-placed merchandise can be a great revenue generator for your yoga business by giving your students a chance to show their love for your brand. For example, you could design and sell a Rock Your Chakras T-shirt.

Trainings

The type of training we are all most familiar with is the 200- or 300-hour teacher training; however, this is not the only kind of training that exists. There are both teacher trainings and specialty trainings. What they have in common is that each consists of at least 12 hours of programming and that each requires the highest commitment from you in terms of planning, marketing, and facilitating. It takes a substantial amount of time to develop the content and to lead these programs. By the time a student is ready to spend this much time and money with you, they are loyal and committed to your business, which is why I consider training another way to marry the market.

Specialty training is for teachers or students who want to learn more about a specific aspect of yoga—for example, a 50-hour training in chakra yoga sequencing for already-trained teachers or a 50-hour sadhana specialty training for students who want to master their home practice. Teacher training, on the other hand, is a specific type of product within the training service model. Teacher trainings are programs that teach and certify students to become yoga teachers. This particular product is important in the yoga space because it develops the most committed relationships of all the service models. It's like creating a family within the market, and just like raising a family, teacher training requires an extremely high commitment to planning and execution, and it carries a high burden of responsibility because your teacher training graduates are byproducts of you. By training others to teach yoga, you become a teacher trainer, and part of your business becomes a yoga school.

How much responsibility you have for your graduates depends on your strategy. Some teacher trainers feel responsible only through the time of graduation and prefer to let their graduates go out and make their way in the world with no attachment to the yoga school. Other teacher trainers like to keep their graduates, or "children," in the nest and part of the yoga school as members of a family with a shared goal. Some teacher training programs last for years before the teacher trainer deems that the student is ready to teach that particular style of yoga, and some programs last a month. There is a debate in the industry about how long a teacher training program should last to adequately train a teacher. Regardless of how you envision your teacher training program coming to life, becoming a teacher trainer can be a natural part of your yoga business. But keep in mind that it often takes many years before a yoga teacher is ready to consider training others.

In addition, when your students graduate, it is important to have continuing education (any of the service models can be used for continuing education) built into your business offerings for graduates from your yoga school to be able to continue to develop and hone their craft. Most experienced teachers will tell you that they never stop learning, so training someone to teach doesn't mean that their learning from you is finished.

Note that your yoga school can be registered through the Yoga Alliance, although it does not have to be. We will discuss this in more detail in chapter 6.

Retreats

A retreat is an immersion that takes place on the road. These are full-day, full-weekend, or multiday experiences that typically take place outside of the yoga studio. These are higher-priced programs that require substantially more investment in time and money from your students as well as substantially more investment in preparation and delivery from you. By the time someone trusts you enough to go somewhere with you, you have definitely put a ring on it, so I consider the retreat service model a marriage to the market. Retreats can provide an exciting and adventurous element to your business by providing a way to keep existing clients clamoring for something new. We will explore the best practices for retreats in chapter 6.

Your Yoga Business Homework

Consider the Service Models

Take a moment here to consider the service models—one-to-ones, group sessions, conferences or festivals, workshops, immersions, trainings, retreats—by answering the following questions:

Which of the service models resonates most with you and why? You can have more than one.

____

____

What questions do you have about these service models? ______________________________

____

____

Which of the service models resonates least with you and why? ______________________________

____

____

Which of the service models did you find most surprising when you learned more about it and why? ______________________________

____

____

I imagine that by now your mind is whirling as you start figuring out which business type you want to adopt and which new service models you want to develop. It's all quite exciting because it's all possible! In the following chapters we will dig further into each service model to help you decide which you will pursue. Information will be provided for how to run each service model, so you will have a firm foundation for creating, maintaining, or developing your yoga business.

5

ONE-TO-ONE AND GROUP SESSIONS

One-to-one and group sessions are the service models every yoga teacher uses to begin building their yoga business, and these are often the service models that remain constant throughout their career. One-to-one and group sessions are extremely important because they are the first opportunity you have to engage with your customers, and as you know, first impressions really do matter. Many customers you meet in one-to-one or group sessions will become lifelong consumers of your entire menu of products and services.

ONE-TO-ONE SESSIONS

Yoga was originally designed to be taught in a one-to-one setting, using an individualized approach that tailors the teachings, practices, and asanas to a single student based on their unique needs as recommended by their teacher. One-to-one teaching was the first type of teacher-to-student relationship and has historically been a foundational service model for yoga teachers since Krishnamacharya was working one-on-one with the Maharaja.

We are a long way from the 1940s in a private room in the Maharaja's palace. In modern times before the COVID-19 pandemic, some yoga students practiced vinyasa flow yoga to loud music with 50 students packed into a single classroom. Even though some yoga teachers and students would not dare to "get their yoga on" in any way other than in a large group class, I believe that teaching one-to-one yoga will always be an essential part of a yoga business.

In 2020, the pandemic brought a huge shift to the way people accepted and partook in one-to-one sessions. In-person doctor and therapist visits became telehealth calls and videoconference therapy sessions, while in-person group and one-to-one yoga sessions also migrated online. There was an overall increase in demand for online guidance and instruction, whether it was for yoga, mentoring, or health coaching.

Many teachers find that the one-to-one service model allows for easier time and lifestyle management because they can control their day-to-day schedule.

Many teachers find that the one-to-one service model allows for easier time and lifestyle management because they can control their day-to-day schedule. This is in comparison, of course, to the group class service model, which typically requires them to teach according to the studio's needs. One-to-ones can be scheduled to the teacher's and their client's needs. Many teachers also love the one-to-one service model because it gives them ample time and space to create an in-depth relationship with a student.

I know some yoga teachers who do not offer one-to-one sessions because of the limitations of scale. If you spend an hour or more with just one person, you can't spend that time anywhere else or with anyone else, which limits how many students you can reach in a day. It is also limiting because some students simply don't like the intimacy and the expectations that exist between the teacher and the student when there are just two in the relationship. I also know many teachers who thrive on offering only one-to-one sessions—many of whom have a six-figure income. They set their prices well and go deep into individualizing for each client. And then there's the rest of us who use one-to-ones as part but not all of our yoga business.

Real Talk

"I teach [high-end] private yoga classes because I am committed to healing one person at a time and prospering as a solopreneur and radical philanthropist. When I left law to teach yoga full time, I had a profound understanding of the value of time. While many people think about an hourly rate, my clients pay me for results. I crafted an extraordinary six-figure business model where I freed myself from the corporate yoga organizations and shifted the locus of control to me, myself, and I."
Nicole Payseur
Private and corporate yoga instructor

Whether one-to-ones are already a huge part of your business or you are considering making it a larger part of your business, let's take a look at some tried-and-tested techniques to create, maintain, and level up your one-to-one business.

Create Your One-to-One Business

This section provides best practices for yoga professionals who are thinking about starting or who are in the early stages of building out their one-to-one yoga service model. These best practices are intended to help you understand what the one-to-one service model is like and to help you set yourself up for success.

Seek advice.

Before beginning to teach one-to-one, ask questions about the one-to-one service model and gather best practices from other yoga teachers. Ideally, you would speak with at least two yoga teachers who have different amounts of experience and teach in different geographic locations so you get well-rounded advice. It's always helpful to find out as much as you can about a new endeavor before you begin.

Take a test drive.

Not sure what you think about one-to-ones in person or online? Then take a test drive and work with real-life clients. Give yourself a chance to figure out how you feel about teaching one-to-one rather than acting off how you think you'll feel about teaching one-to-one. Before the pandemic, I'd say 90 percent of the yoga teachers I worked with were not comfortable with teaching one-to-one online. Mind you, they had never actually done it, but they were sure it wasn't for them. I had a good laugh as I fielded calls from teachers around the world who I had urged to start teaching yoga online years earlier who were finally forced because of circumstance to teach yoga one-to-one online. And wouldn't you know, they ended up loving it. There's nothing more enlightening than doing something to help you form an educated opinion.

A great way to find students to take a test drive with you is to invite friends and family or longtime group session students to free or discounted one-to-one sessions. Your time is valuable, of course, but the intent of these test drives isn't to make money; it's to see whether this service model is right for you. You don't want to sit around waiting for your first one-to-one session while you are determining whether you want to develop this area of your business. You'd be surprised how many yoga teachers get stuck in this very place. Offering a one-to-one session for free or at a discounted rate will allow you to gather the information you need quickly, which means that if this is a service model you want to develop, you will be on your way to full-price sessions faster if you have test driven with a few clients.

Work your network.

Growing a one-to-one business relies heavily on word-of-mouth referrals, and yoga professionals typically do not mine their existing network as efficiently as they could. A simple strategy to work your network is to ask existing clients for testimonials that you can share on your website or via social media. People inherently love to follow and support a highly recommended or reviewed product. People also love to share about or recommend a product that they love, especially if they get rewarded for it. Consider asking your existing network for a list of people they know that they can refer you to. Perhaps they will earn a reward like a free one-to-one session, an item of merchandise, or a discount off a workshop or training for every referral they make. The possibilities are endless.

Get a commitment.

Another great way to grow your one-to-one business is to ask your clients to commit to a package of sessions (some teachers only work one-to-one with clients who purchase packages, at least after the first few sessions). Remind your clients of the benefits of consistent yoga practice, especially related to their direct goals. Are they looking to be able to meditate for longer, nail that arm balance, or be less reactive at home with their partner or kids? Demonstrate for your client how spending more time with you will allow them to reach their direct goals and offer them a one-to-one package that meets those needs. We will talk about pricing and packaging more in depth in chapter 8.

Maintain Your One-to-One Business

This section provides best practices for yoga professionals already operating a one-to-one business and looking for ways to keep current clients happy, engaged, and wanting to spend more time and money with your business. Let's look at strategies for maintaining your existing one-to-one business.

Create feedback loops.

When you have been in business for a while, especially if things are going well, you tend not to think about what you could be doing better or differently. It's a form of complacency that seasoned entrepreneurs regularly fall into. And who can blame you, when you have worked so hard to build your business, for wanting to coast a bit and let the momentum simply keep rolling on its own? However, because you are here to take your yoga business further, I suggest you create a feedback loop by contacting your existing, satisfied clients and asking them about the service you're currently providing and how you could improve it. Not only will you come up with a great list of innovations, but you will also reengage your existing client base by letting them know that you care about the service you are providing and, more importantly, their opinions of it.

Create boundaries.

There's no doubt that running a one-to-one business is intimate. You're spending time alone with a client, in your space or theirs, oftentimes discussing personal matters and having your physical bodies in close proximity. There is an inherent difficulty in this type of environment in creating and maintaining effective boundaries. I have found that some of the most successful one-to-one businesses create serious boundaries! These boundaries may address scheduling, how payments are collected, when the client does or does not have access to you, the location of the one-to-ones, and more. For example, using an online scheduler to book your appointments, send appointment reminders, and send feedback surveys or using an online payment portal to collect payments on singles and subscriptions helps to create a professional boundary. Imagine what your one-to-one business would look and feel like if you no longer collected cash in hand or casually confirmed appointments with clients via text message?

There are many great web-based tools and software for adding professional-level processes to your one-to-one business. Don't be afraid to upgrade or automate your processes no matter how long you have been doing things the old-fashioned way in your one-to-one business. When you upgrade or automate, be sure to take the time to explain new business processes to clients to reduce frustration and keep them satisfied.

Another area where boundaries become loose is the client relationship. As the client relationship deepens, many one-to-one facilitators find themselves in situations where clients want to talk or check in between their scheduled sessions. Failing to set boundaries with out-of-session time decreases your rate because you put in more time with the client for the same pay, and many teachers lose a lot of value in their business this way. A strategy to limit the time in which you allow clients access to you is to offer scheduled office time as part of your one-to-one offering. This means that you set the time when you can be available for phone calls, texts, or email exchanges and roll the cost of that time into their package of one-to-ones. For example, if your office hours are Monday from noon to 1 p.m., and you can assume that your client will reach out to you once a week for 15 minutes, you can build the cost of one additional hour into their package for the month. Perhaps your one-to-one rate is $100, so you would sell a monthly membership for $500 that includes four one-to-one sessions and one office hour. This creates a boundary by putting a price tag and a set schedule on the access your clients have to you. The truth is, poor professional boundaries make it difficult to run the business like a business, and as you will see later, a large part of leveling up your one-to-one business and taking it to the next level is making it more businesslike.

Keep packaging fresh.

A great strategy for keeping existing clients interested is to continuously create fresh one-to-one packages. Each of your one-to-one packages might have a similar price for a certain number of sessions, but you can get creative from there. For instance, you can include a nutrition consultation, discounts at a local health food store or eatery, admission to a workshop by a teacher you admire, or even create packages around seasonal themes such as a New Year's bootcamp. We will dive deeper into ways to diversify your packages in chapter 8, Menu of Services.

Use expiration dates to your advantage.

I recommend that one-to-one packages expire after a certain amount of time. There's nothing worse than chasing a client to use the sessions that they've paid for, or them showing up wanting to redeem unused sessions or get a refund years after their purchase date. If you don't feel comfortable making a general rule about expiration dates, you can ask clients at the time of purchase what they feel is a reasonable date by which to have completed all the sessions. This creates a supreme level of commitment and accountability. Discussing the expiration date together can also be a motivating way to set a goal that encourages them to keep a consistent pace with their sessions and keeps them purchasing new packages of sessions regularly.

Make your schedule work for you, not just for your clients.

Many teachers are too flexible when it comes to scheduling with their clients, which usually comes from a fear of losing business. Many yoga teachers think that the best way to sell more one-to-one sessions is to be infinitely available and to let the clients set the schedule, rather than steering clients to the appointment times that work best for you as the service provider. There is nothing wrong with limiting your availability. It may seem counterintuitive when you want to have *more* business to be *less* available, but let's think it through. Which do you find yourself drawn to: yoga classes and restaurants that you know space is hard to come by or those that have an empty book of reservations and are always easy to get into? It's an old economic principle that scarcity breeds demand, and the same logic applies to your one-to-one business. In addition, it's better for your overall workweek to have a set schedule of time blocked for delivery of one-to-one sessions. Remember, you need

Busy yoga teachers do it all, including toting their own props to and from events, as seen in this photo of Erica Garcia Abergel.

Your Yoga Business Homework

Book a One-to-One Session

Book and take a one-to-one session either in person or online so you can have the one-to-one experience as a student rather than as a yoga teacher. You can take a session with someone you know or anonymously, but allow yourself to go through the complete process from shopping, to purchasing, to completing the session as if you were a student taking a one-to-one session for the first time. Make notes about what you love and don't love about the experience, and make notes about which of the one-to-one best practices you can see in action. This activity is one part inspiration, one part critique, and wholly necessary.

Available online on HK*Propel*.

time for working on your business as well as in it, and promoting your availability helps ensure that you can move from function to function. It may be scary to say no to someone who doesn't fit into your schedule or to counteroffer and suggest a time that is different from what they originally asked for, but the alternative is that you are always available and saying yes to every client at every time of day and every day of the week. You can see how that would create chaos for your calendar, your business, and your life.

Level Up Your One-to-One Business

This section consists of best practices to truly professionalize your one-to-one business.

Create policies with penalties.

A great way to level up your one-to-one business is by making it a professional enterprise and creating policies with penalties. Although many yoga business owners are uncomfortable creating policies because the structure seems constrictive, policies create freedom in your business. Lack of structure in your one-to-one business is the wrong way to develop long-term growth and stability.

I strongly suggest you set policies with penalties in your one-to-one business, especially when it comes to cancellations, lateness, and expirations. For example, if a client is late and you teach over the scheduled session end time to ensure that they get a full session, not only have you spent extra time on this client without getting extra payment for that time, but worse yet, your niceness will not encourage them to be on time. A policy of ending sessions at their scheduled end time and not teaching past that will penalize the client and discourage the behavior.

Or if a client cancels with short notice, and you allow them to use the session at a later date—guess who's more likely to cancel on short notice again? But if there is a penalty in place for canceling on short notice, such as losing the session, you will discourage the behavior. Don't worry about having too many policies in place, because the list of exceptions and leniencies typically allowed in your businesses will be long. Each nicety—a few minutes here and a few minutes there—all ultimately cost you money. Having policies with penalties will help you offset these costs. In addition, having policies with penalties creates an air of mutual respect because your clients will know that you mean business. And you do, don't you?

I also suggest that you clearly list your policies with penalties on your website and marketing materials, and make sure that your new clients have had a look before purchasing. Some yoga teachers even have clients click a box to confirm they've read the policies before they purchase. In your effort to level up, you can also go back to long-term clients and introduce them to your new policies with penalties. They may be reluctant at first, but if they know that the changes are to secure the longevity of your business (you can tell them why you are implementing the new policies), they will usually be supportive—even if you need to raise your prices.

Refresh your pricing.

Speaking of raising prices, remember to keep your pricing fresh. As the market shifts and changes, your prices should shift and change, too. On occasion, it is okay to grandfather a handful of long-term clients (meaning they are allowed to pay the original price when you raise prices for others). But many yoga teachers know that their prices no longer reflect the true value of their time yet still regularly charge new clients old prices. It's one thing to be afraid to give an old client a new price, but to give a new client an old price just doesn't make business sense. As you will see in your assessment in chapter 9, a slight price increase on all of your services for the number of clients you have right now can have a huge impact on your bottom line. Moderate price increases (less than 30 percent) are highly unlikely to cause turnover. For instance, I recently paid $30 for a drop-in yoga class in New York City. Before the pandemic, the price was $22, and asking for $30 would have been unheard of. I happily paid the $30; I understood that because of the pandemic, class size was severely limited, which meant the price per student should have increased to make up for the lower number of students.

Market conditions and realities affect businesses all the time, which means that your prices can be reflexive in response. For instance, you might move to a new neighborhood, increasing the travel time and cost of getting to your existing clients. Rather than taking a hit and making less money per private session, you can raise your prices appropriately and let your clients know why your prices are increasing.

Make the most of the Zoom boom.

Another fantastic way to level up your one-to-one business is by harnessing the reach of the Internet. Most yoga teachers used to be hesitant about teaching online—mostly because they didn't believe that high-quality yoga experiences could be had through a screen and they were intimidated by the technology. I believe we all know now that you can indeed have deep and meaningful yoga experiences online. Teaching online allows you to connect powerfully with the global marketplace, including those you may never have the opportunity to meet in person, such as your social media followers. We will explore creating a great virtual classroom in chapter 7.

Your Yoga Business Homework

Take Stock of Your One-to-One Business

Have a look at the list of best practices we have covered in this one-to-one section, and mark those you are already using in your business. Write down ideas you have on how to incorporate these strategies or how to use these strategies more effectively in your one-to-one business no matter whether you are creating, maintaining, or leveling up. I find that nearly all yoga businesses can use each strategy no matter how developed they are.

_____ Seek advice: ______________________________

____

____

____

_____ Take a test drive: ______________________________

____

____

____

_____ Work your network: ______________________________

____

____

____

_____ Get a commitment: ______________________________

____

____

____

_____ Create feedback loops: ______________________________

____

____

____

_____ Create boundaries: ______________________________

____

____

____

(continued)

Your Yoga Business Homework *(continued)*

_____ Keep packaging fresh: ______________________________

_____ Use expiration dates to your advantage: ______________________________

_____ Make your schedule work for you, not just for your clients: ______________________________

_____ Create policies with penalties: ______________________________

_____ Refresh your pricing: ______________________________

_____ Make the most of the Zoom boom: ______________________________

GROUP SESSIONS

In chapter 1, I shared about my first yoga class, and when I think back on my 20 years of practice, I can remember so many life-changing group class sessions—experiences that changed me mentally, physically, and emotionally in 90 minutes. It's amazing the amount of awakening that can transpire in a single group session.

The group sessions you teach are where the majority of the students who will become loyal to you will initially get to know you, where you will build trust and rapport with them, and where they will decide whether they will continue to study with you or not. Through the group experience, they will decide whether they will take a one-to-one session with you; attend your workshop, immersion, retreat, or training; stay subscribed online; and so on.

The first date you have with your students is in a group session, and I know you know how great an opportunity a first date is to make a good impression and to set the tone for the future of the relationship. I also know that you know that people who have a bad first date usually don't have a second one. Great group sessions are vital to your business by keeping your pipeline of students full. Group sessions are also where most yoga teachers begin their careers, and as they journey and diversify into other areas of their businesses, they often overlook the opportunity to level up this most essential building block of their business.

Many household name teachers place great focus on group classes within their larger yoga business, offering a refined product and a well-branded experience. Most household name yoga teachers will tell you that perfecting the group session experience is key to the studio's success.

Great group sessions are memorable experiences.

Some of us have been teaching group sessions the same way for so long that thinking fresh is now vital to our business's longevity. There's a fine line between finding something that works and being consistent about delivering it, and stagnating. While your relationship with your group session changes over the course of your career—the format, type, delivery, quantity, location, technology—the importance remains the same. If you want to keep increasing the number of "marriage proposals" you receive, the number of loyal clients you have, and the higher-ticket products you sell, you have to keep going on first dates. So let's look at best practices for amazing group sessions.

Make it memorable.

There are many ways you can make your group session memorable. For example, you can open and close your classes with a familiar chant, salutation, or tagline. I loved chanting the Anusara invocation at the beginning of class back in the early 2000s; it was one part blessing and one part branding, and I couldn't wait to be back in class to sing it again. The consistency and familiarity created a memorable experience, and, of course, the repetition of the invocation had a magic of its own. The beginning and end of a group session are prime opportunities to create memorable moments, as are all the other moments in between.

I like to consider memorable experiences in other industries, like music or food. What is it about the experience of watching your favorite band or dining at your favorite restaurant that keeps you coming back for more? Find ways to re-create those feelings and mimic those experiences in your group sessions. For instance, if your favorite restaurant always gives a small chocolate at the end of dinner, perhaps once a month give out a small chocolate at the end of class. Or if your favorite band is known for playing a certain song in every concert, perhaps you play a certain song in every class. There are many ways to re-create and mimic memorable experiences in other industries in your group sessions.

Be on a first-name basis.

Make it your business to know every student by name; it matters! This little bit of personal attention helps your students feel special and seen by you, so do your absolute best here. Some teachers ask everyone to write their name on tape on their mats, and others make sure that their Zoom profiles have their first names and pronouns visible. It may seem awkward to ask in the beginning, but the result is worth it.

Keep your material fresh.

Consistency is key to a memorable group experience, but you can have too much of a good thing. Being repetitive may be a new strategy, or you may need to ask yourself when you last came up with new material for your group sessions. Imagine if your favorite band played the same set list of songs and you went to the concert three times a week—there really can be too much of a good thing. Are you teaching on autopilot, or have you been cracking the exact same joke for years? Your effort to incorporate fresh ideas into your group sessions should be intentional, and you can make it an annual task. It will also happen organically if you continuously seek out new experiences like taking classes from other teachers and in different physical modalities or emotional therapies, exploring art forms like music and painting, and continuing to read and research topics that are dear to you. Even your most regular students can benefit from a refresher of the information that is most important to you as a teacher. You can go back to the beginning or go deeper into the content with them and spend more time working slowly though each concept. Keeping your material fresh doesn't mean it has to be brand new—it can also be delivering old content in a new way.

Your Yoga Business Homework

Book a Group Session

Book and take three group sessions either in person or online so you have the experience of the student, rather than the yoga teacher. You can take sessions with someone you know or anonymously, but allow yourself to go through the complete process from shopping, to purchasing, to taking the session as if you were a student. Make notes about what you love and don't love about the experience. It is also really cool to take a session with a teacher you have known or practiced with for a very long time, a teacher whose jokes you know by heart. It is interesting to note how even they may or may not be keeping it fresh. This activity is one part inspiration, one part critique, and wholly necessary.

Available online on HK*Propel*.

Create a class schedule that works for *you*.

Many yoga teachers dread their group sessions because the schedule isn't ideal for their lifestyle. If you are going to own this service model, you need your class schedule to be manageable at the least and exciting at the most. What parts of your group session schedule are working for you and what parts are working against you? What changes could you make to your schedule to make it even more ideal?

It's best to make your schedule work for you because, like it or not, in order to be successful at group sessions, you need to show up as often as possible and minimize the need to sub. Showing up builds trust, trust builds loyalty, and loyalty builds a following. It's hard to fall in love with someone who is a no-show, so show up as often as you can for yourself, your students, and your business. Better to set a small schedule of classes that you can commit to than one so extensive you can't manage to attend all your classes. Plus, a schedule that you are 100 percent committed to, even if it is small, will eventually yield greater results.

Showing up also allows you to be a true part of the community through sharing the same space and a common interest, and community is one of the most beautiful aspects of yoga. The less time you're present, the less you'll be able to benefit from the community. Yes, more group sessions immediately equals more money, but a more committed presence in fewer places will help you make more money in the long run as you leverage the community and build the loyalty needed for those students to participate in the rest of your yoga business.

Offer support.

Speak with your students after class about their individual needs and challenges. Being able to provide a few minutes of additional support outside of class is a winning strategy. Remember, you are not a therapist, and appropriate boundaries help keep a professional relationship healthy—so give a little time, but not too much. Yoga teacher Matt Giordano also loves to give a little sample of what he will teach in an upcoming workshop after class—just enough to whet the appetite, but not so much that he gives away all the goods for free.

Remember you are delivering a product.

It is important to remember that your group sessions are a product. Your students are paying you for an experience, and they have expectations about what that experience will be. This means that being prepared and planning well to deliver a good experience matters. No one wants a hastily prepared session, and both you and your students deserve your best. Thinking about your group session like you are delivering a product is akin to serving a patron at a restaurant. You've marketed to them, they like your menu, and they have reserved a spot and walked in. The space is clean and beautiful upon their arrival, with music playing to create ambience. The chef has been preparing all morning and has sourced the best ingredients, has tried the dish herself, and is mentally ready to cook. I think you can see in the comparison that each step of the preparation process and delivery process contributes to the delivery of a great dining experience, and it is the same for your group sessions. Arriving early, cleaning and beautifying your space, creating the ambience, planning and trying your class plan in advance, and being mentally prepared and ready to teach are all simple and effective ways to deliver a great product.

Be you.

In chapter 2, we learned that the best branding is to be more you, and that extends to the product that you deliver in the classroom. It takes a long time to teach like yourself, and in the beginning, being a good emulator is important. However, there is a difference between emulating someone's teaching style and emulating their persona. Because of this confusion, many teachers pretend to be someone they're not, even down to the sound and intonation of their teaching voice. This inauthenticity will disappoint your students, who have fallen in love with a false version of you. Plus, it's exhausting to do all that pretending.

Keep your eye on your *why*.

Remember to reinforce your purpose by sharing it with your students when you can. Depending on your teaching platform and style, you will have more or less time for these conversations with integrity within the group class experience. Sharing your purpose isn't about pushing your agenda as much as it is about weaving what's important to you into your classes on a consistent basis. For example, if you notice that you have a group session full of first-time students, you may start the group session with *why* and tell your story of why you began teaching.

Be professional.

You wouldn't show up to a professional job interview with wrinkly clothes or smoothie on your face, would you? As a yoga teacher, you are in a position of power, and I strongly suggest that you look the part and take your seat with pride. Give yourself time to prepare, time to get to class, and time to exit. You are delivering a product, and are in the front of the room as a leader, a person the students look up to and respect. An air of professionalism helps students take you seriously, which develops into respect for you and your business. When you take yourself seriously, they will too. Taking pride in your job (be careful not to mix this up with arrogance) helps to create a winning experience in class time and time again.

Your Yoga Business Homework

Journal Your Most Memorable Sessions

With all of your one-to-one and group sessions, think about what keeps you coming back and your most powerful yoga experiences and teachers. What were the magical moments of your experience? What did they say that was profound? How did they hold space in the room? What was their teaching like? What little things did they do? And also think back to your worst experiences—events that left a bad taste in your mouth and the teachers and studios to which you have never returned. What was it that left such a bad impression on that first date? Write down your responses to these questions. The notes are important to keep in mind as you create, maintain, and level up your one-to-one and group sessions.

Available online on HK*Propel*.

As you can see, one-to-one and group sessions are very rich and versatile service models worthy of considerable time and attention and capable of generating some serious income. In the next chapter, we will head into the large-format service models: workshops, trainings, immersions, and retreats.

6

WORKSHOPS, TRAININGS, IMMERSIONS, AND RETREATS

Over the years, I have supported many yoga teachers in developing workshops, trainings, immersions, and retreats, which I refer to as large-format programs. These yoga services allowed them an opportunity to diversify their business by adding higher-priced products. I've supported everything from the conceptualization of the events and booking the venues, to opening the front doors to greet students each day; I have even been responsible for making sure that the toilet paper didn't run out. I've coordinated and implemented detailed marketing plans, handled student registration and compliance with the Yoga Alliance, monitored the students' dietary needs—pretty much everything you can think of from start to finish other than teaching them myself. Each large-format program was unique in the reason it existed, who it was for, and how and where it was delivered, yet there were common tools and strategies that I found useful in each and every workshop, training, immersion, and retreat that I am excited to share with you.

WORKSHOPS

Creating and leading workshops is one of the first steps you will take toward diversifying your yoga business. It is exciting when teachers expand into this service model because it is usually the first indication of the direction in which their business will evolve. Through the creation of a workshop, you will have identified a topic that is important enough to you that you want to share it in a deeper way with students. You may lead workshops at studios where you teach regularly or as an invited guest presenter at another studio or venue.

Workshops are great revenue generators because the additional time that you spend with students allows you to charge a higher price than a standard group session. While you cannot lead a workshop every day or more than once a week in the same way you are able to teach standard group classes, you can hold these special group sessions regularly. One weekend a month is an ideal schedule to aspire to if you want to maximize this service model, but once a quarter can also be quite fruitful.

Many yoga teachers do not use the workshop service model, or they do not use it well. Here are things to think about when considering how you can further develop workshops within your yoga business.

Real Talk

"I would have workshops of four or five people, and I just had to keep plugging away. You gotta just keep on plugging."
Anodea Judith
Author, public speaker, and therapist

You already know enough.

Many yoga teachers delay their use of the workshop service model because they don't think that they know enough to begin; however, if you know enough to teach a great group session, you know enough to teach a great workshop. Many yoga teachers also overteach their workshops in an effort to compensate for a perceived lack of knowledge—meaning they cover a ton of information to make it seem like they know more. I suggest a less-is-more approach because a little information can go a long way, and some of the simpler concepts of your teaching will still be revolutionary to your students. You can build an entire workshop around a singular concept and go deep into it. This gives students time to grasp and integrate the materials because the focus is clear and concise. Choose a single topic that you know well, and create the plan for your workshop around it. Remember, reinforcement of concepts is a good thing! For instance, you may choose a topic such as how changing your breathing patterns in familiar poses changes how they feel, or your topic may be how reaching outward in familiar poses or hugging inward toward the midline in familiar poses changes how they feel. You can lead an entire workshop on chaturanga, tadasana, or understanding the importance of savasana—even the most basic elements of your yoga practice are deep wells of possibility.

Make your workshop yours.

Often when developing workshop content, yoga teachers veer away from their pillars and lead workshops that they see other yoga teachers leading, such as the ever-popular topic of inversions, even though inversions may not be a pillar of their business or even part of their personal practice. In this instance, yoga teachers overteach their workshops to compensate for a lack of knowledge. If you focus on teaching from the pillars of your practice, then you will know enough without reaching. Remember that you run a yoga business and that every opportunity you have to teach is an opportunity to strengthen your business. Lean into your pillars for workshop topics, and if you do choose a popular topic such as inversions, approach the topic through the lens of one of your pillars. For instance, if empowerment is one of your pillars, your inversion workshop could be about making your inversion work for you and could focus on modifications and deep inquiry into what feels good in your body rather than flinging yourself upside down any time you are asked.

Combine your content.

As shared in chapter 4, a workshop is a great opportunity to combine your content—for example, a class and a lecture. The wonderful thing about workshops is the additional time you have with your students, so feel free to play with different kinds of content in one time period. I love it when a teacher lectures, reads, and allows for group discussion of a topic before we experience it in the practice. It's a bit of an academic approach to learning to be exposed to a topic in a cerebral way as well as in a physical way. Think back to all of the programs you have offered over the years—these bits and bobs of content can be woven together into a great workshop.

Building a Workshop Tour

YAMA runs a booking agency for yoga teachers who conduct classes at yoga studios, conferences, and festivals worldwide. Just like a rock band, many of our teachers are constantly "on tour." A successful tour requires managing logistics, including travel, lodging, marketing, promotions, and expenses. A tour is built around an anchor date, a booking that has been scheduled and contracted, by creating a schedule from that date and location that allows the teacher to physically get from point A to point B easily and at the lowest possible cost.

Typically, the workshop touring process starts by leading successful workshops in your hometown and then taking those programs on the road. The success you build in your hometown allows you to build credibility and earn the trust of host venues. Bringing in a guest yoga teacher from outside a studio is risky and time consuming. Your host venues will feel much more confident booking you if you have a successful track record elsewhere; don't be surprised if a host venue asks you for the attendance numbers of your most recent workshop.

Host venues have a variety of reasons to seek a guest teacher:

- *Financially motivated studios* host guest teachers that they know will fill the room to capacity.
- *Experience-motivated studios* host guest teachers that will bring a fresh perspective and excitement to the studio.
- *Educationally motivated studios* host senior guest teachers that bring depth and lineage, even if they have to cover the fees and expenses.

Rarely will you find a studio that wants to take a big risk on hosting a yoga teacher. So build, build, build at home. It takes multiple workshops at the same host studio to build word of mouth and gain the traction that leads to high attendance. It's easier to put in the time, energy, and resources to build when the venues are closer to home.

It will take time for workshop touring to recover after the COVID-19 pandemic because hosting guest teachers is not an essential service model for most businesses. Many studios have closed or are barely surviving, which makes hosting a workshop a nice thing to do but not necessary. Because venues are less likely to take risks, teachers who want to go on tour need to be entrepreneurial—perhaps rent their own venues or offer to teach workshops online for host venues in order to build demand for an in-person event later when market conditions improve. This is a smart strategy even when the market is stable. It's a less risky way to build community because there are fewer logistics to consider while laying the groundwork for an in-person tour in the future.

For most current household name yoga teachers, extensive touring was vital to building the name recognition that allowed them to attain this level. However, being on the road often isn't as glamorous as it looks on Instagram. Some touring yoga teachers do not unpack their suitcases, or they end up being away from their families for extended lengths of time. And, of course, when on the road, they have to deal with the ups and downs of modern travel, Mother Nature, civil unrest, pandemics, and fluctuations in the value of currency.

Touring yoga teachers also have to consider visas and entry requirements. It is important to be mindful of the requirements for working out of state or out of the country. In the past, touring yoga teachers could ignore visa and entry requirements, but now that yoga is mainstream and it is so easy to research someone's persona online, you must be properly documented and legally allowed to earn money in the state or country that you are traveling to. There are horror stories of yoga teachers being sent home by airport security because they had no entry paperwork, often leaving full rooms of disappointed students or retreat attendees.

Do not be discouraged—smart workshop touring rocks and creates revenue and memorable experiences. Start small and local, and create work habits and infrastructure for keeping an eye on the details and your bottom line. As attendance numbers grow, your invitations to teach will extend wider and wider.

TRAININGS, IMMERSIONS, AND RETREATS

In chapter 4 we reviewed trainings, immersions, and retreats as service models—what they are and what to think about as you decide whether to incorporate these service models into your yoga business and how you will do it. Now we will look at my hard-earned tips, tools, and best practices for trainings, immersions, and retreats.

To do or not to do?

As I stated earlier, large-format programs are a lot of work. You need to ask yourself whether you really want to take this on because the heavy workload is not for everyone. Many yoga business owners do not find value in these in-depth and intense experiences that require a large investment of time and energy in the planning phases as well as teaching and hosting. If you aren't sure what you think, assist at someone else's large-format program or volunteer to be on staff to gain experience. If that isn't possible, at the very least, sit down with a mentor to learn about their experiences with large-format programming. I am sure they have a lot of valuable insight.

Assist or volunteer at someone else's event to gain experience.

Partner up to create content.

Large-format programs require a lot of time in front of the room teaching, and I often see yoga teachers work together to produce these programs. It's a smart way to collaborate. Who can you partner with to help support the teaching schedule or provide other activities on the agenda? Typically, you need to be the star of your program, meaning teach the bulk of the hours. Having a solid lineup of guest teachers or activity hosts can keep things interesting and keep you fresh. You do not need to be the expert at everything, and even if you are an expert at everything (I hope you're smiling), hiring someone who can take on a particular component of your content and do it well could be a good investment. For instance, just because you *can* lead anatomy in your training doesn't mean you *have* to. Partnering with others to cover the content is a smart way to build more efficient large-format programs. Be sure to include the fees for the guest teachers in your event calculator (discussed later in this chapter) to make sure it is an investment your event can afford.

Determine your purpose for the program.

Are you holding this event to have a good time yourself or to provide a good time for your students? (We had such a blast in Tuscany that it was worth taking a financial loss, but we didn't plan it that way! See the sidebar Learning From My Own Mistakes on page 63.) Is revenue your main reason why, or is it to provide in-depth education or to give back to the community? When planning a large-format program, it is important (as always) to think about *why* you want to create the program. Your reason why will affect your decisions on location, vibe, pricing, marketing, the daily schedule, and so on.

Deliver results and meet expectations.

Knowing your purpose will help you to create a successful experience for your attendees. Ask yourself what the desired outcome of your program is. What do you want the students to walk away with, to experience, or to understand conceptually? What do you want them to be able to achieve physically? What kind of impact do you want to have on them? Great large-format programs have a clear arc and a clear goal. If I sign up for 50-hour sadhana training and have been told I will develop tools to help me master a home practice, then as a student, I expect that I will get that. You'd be surprised how many programs do not meet the expectations that they set. If you want to keep people coming back, you must deliver results and meet expectations.

Think like the student.

I recommend thinking about large-format programs from the perspective of the students. Think through each detail of their experience from the time of sign-up, through their travel, and to the pace of their daily schedule. Think about the opportunities they have to rest, connect with each other, have access to you, and provide feedback. You are not responsible for keeping them happy 100 percent of the time—that's unrealistic and typically a losing game. However, putting yourself in their shoes will go a long way toward helping you care for your attendees and anticipating their needs. These students are committing to you both in time and money, and thinking through each detail of their experience will help you build a great large-format program.

At a maximum, aim to exceed your students' expectations; at a minimum, deliver on what you sold to them.

Get help with the details.

Large-format programs are complex with lots of additional responsibilities besides the teaching itself. Don't be afraid to delegate and get help with administrative details and logistics, such as student questions, registration and collecting payments, curriculum design, daily agendas, travel itineraries, manuals, handouts, and on-site hosting—just to name a few. Many yoga teachers never attempt large-format programs because the amount of organizing and number of details can be overwhelming. In fact, the burden is so significant that some companies specialize in handling the details and logistics for trainings, immersions, and retreats. If you'd like to outsource the administration so you can focus on what you do best—teaching and marketing—that option is available to you.

Registering My Programs With Yoga Alliance

By training other teachers to teach yoga, you become a teacher trainer, and part of your business becomes what is known as a yoga school. Your yoga school can be registered through the Yoga Alliance (YA), although it does not have to be and a lot of yoga teachers question the necessity of registration with the Yoga Alliance because of political or financial considerations. I suggest that if you are not a household name teacher with more than 25 years of teaching experience—which indicates in itself that you are qualified as a teacher—that you register yourself and your yoga school with YA. Membership in the Yoga Alliance is a way to verify the quality of your program. Because most yoga students have five years of experience practicing yoga or less, it is a beginner's market, and meeting this quality standard is important for making your clients feel safe. Registering with YA won't negatively affect your business, and will likely be an additional selling point for your teacher training and specialty training.

In addition, once registered with YA and qualified as a continuing education unit (CEU) provider, you can register your programs as eligible for CEUs, which will allow you to market to the YA's community of teachers who need CEUs to fulfill their annual CEU requirements. Not everyone attending a large-format program is there for the hours, but being able to provide CEUs to attendees of your programs is another benefit that will drive business.

MINIMIZING FINANCIAL RISK WITH LARGE-FORMAT PROGRAMS

As an entrepreneur, it is important to minimize risk. Large-format programs offer higher potential reward and higher risk—both in the time and money to bring them to fruition. Many yoga teachers enter poor business arrangements when embarking on large-format programs and take on undue risk such as agreeing to a nonrefundable deposit on a venue or severely underestimating the cost of the time it takes to plan, market, and lead the programs. I have created a few strategies to help you run successful large-format programs with minimal risk.

One strategy I use to minimize risk is to align the payments due to venues with sales goals. In most large-format programs, there are financial commitments that must be made, such as a deposit to reserve the practice space where the event will be held or reserving a block of hotel rooms for your retreat guests. I align the due dates of these financial commitments with sales goals. For example, if you have a 20 percent deposit due to the hotel, set a goal to reach 50 percent of your event sales by the date the deposit is due. This strategy minimizes risk by ensuring that your program is selling well before you need to pay out of pocket. If your program has not reached the sales goal by the date set, you have a safe moment to adjust, renegotiate, and reconsider your plans. Most partners are willing to work with you on aligning the deposits with dates that work well with your sales goals if you are willing to ask.

If you can only make a profit financially with a sold-out event, then you do not have a good business arrangement.

Speaking of sales goals, one of the best ways to minimize risk is to set realistic sales goals. Many yoga business owners wear rose-colored glasses when it comes to sales and registration numbers. I am optimistic (always!) but prefer to set modest sales goals when considering the financial scenario of a large-format program. Your program should make a profit with modest registration. I like for a program to be profitable at 50 to 60 percent capacity.

I created a tool, called the event calculator (see figure 6.1), that helps manage details such as projected expenses, sales goals, ticket price per attendee, percentage splits, and the break-even number of attendees (the number needed to start earning a profit). This calculator is a tool born of necessity and an extraordinary number of yoga events that I have hosted around the globe. I often laugh to myself when reading this chapter, because almost every best practice, feature, and function of the event calculator was a real-life lesson learned during a business interaction between a guest teacher and a host venue or between a teacher trainer or retreat teacher and a student—and usually it was a lesson learned the hard way. It is nice to be able to laugh about those hard-earned learnings years later and to be able to share those lessons with you.

Let's take a closer look at some key items that you must be aware of as you create your own event calculator.

Expenses

Expenses are the costs associated with running your program, and all programs have costs that you can list on the event calculator. These expenses may be your sole responsibility, or they may be shared with others, such as a teaching partner or the host venue. Shared expenses are those that are billed to both you and the other party and are deducted from gross income before any revenue share occurs. Shared expenses are often costs such as venue rental, travel, and marketing expenses. If you are producing the event on your own, you will not have shared expenses.

Some expenses are fixed (will not change), and some expenses are variable (you can adjust what you spend). You can also pad your expenses (list them as more than what you think they will actually cost) or add in a line item for contingency fees to cover unexpected costs. Anticipating expenses in advance will ensure you end up with a predictable bottom line.

Revenue Share and Percentage Splits

A revenue share is a financial arrangement in which each party earns a specific share, or percentage split, of the net income. In the yoga business, 50/50, 60/40, and 70/30 are all common percentage splits. Who gets what is determined by various factors, such as the amount of work each party puts into the event, the expenses required to put on the event, how the marketing duties are shared, and, of course, what each person presents or performs at the event. Make sure you know which split of the revenue share is yours. It is typical that the yoga teacher receives the largest percentage split of the revenue share, although it can vary. Since the COVID-19 pandemic, the percentage splits have fluctuated because expenses have risen, the workload to put on online events is considerably different, and venues need to be more protective of their resources.

FIGURE 6.1 Event Calculator

		Expenses					
Marketing		$0.00					
Handout printing		$0.00					
Travel		$350.00					
Lodging		$0.00					
Ground transport		$0.00					
Room rental		$0.00					
Miscellaneous costs		$0.00					
Total expenses		350.00					
		Goal capacity	**80% capacity**	**60% capacity**	**40% capacity**	**30% capacity**	**25% capacity**
Ticket price	**$220**	26	21	16	10	8	7
Minimum guarantee	**$2,500.00**						
Number of tickets to cover minimum guarantee and expenses	**13**						
Total program gross		5,720.00	4,576.00	3,432.00	2,288.00	1,716.00	1,430.00
Less program expenses		350.00	350.00	350.00	350.00	350.00	350.00
Total program net revenue		5,370.00	4,226.00	3,082.00	1,938.00	1,366.00	1,080.00
Total program net on 70%		3,759.00	2,958.20	2,157.40	1,356.60	956.20	756.00
Total program net on 30%		1,611.00	1,267.80	924.60	581.40	409.80	324.00

Ticket Price

The importance of ticket price to the overall financial success of an event is often underestimated. Depending on how many yoga mats the space holds, which determines the number of tickets you can sell, small variations in the price can make a big difference. The sooner you assess your expenses against anticipated revenue and see how the price of your ticket and total number of tickets available affect what you take home in your percentage split, the better! I create the most thorough event calculator possible before agreeing to put on an event. Sometimes, I find that a venue is too small to turn a profit at our regular ticket price and that I need to sell the event as an intimate experience at a higher price in order to be profitable.

Run the numbers, and then run them again before saying yes to hosting an event.

Your Yoga Business Homework

Create a Sample Workshop, Training, Immersion, or Retreat Calculator

In this activity, you are going to create your own event calculator. First, you will download the event calculator from HK*Propel* (instructions are provided at the front of this book). Once you have the calculator open, begin to input sample expenses, ticket price, and room capacities. The formulas in the event calculator will do the rest of the work for you. If you have recently run a workshop, training, immersion, or retreat in real life, use actual expenses, ticket prices, and room capacities in your calculator.

When looking at the event calculator, first make sure you have included all of the known or possible expenses. Then ask yourself, how does the profit for the event look with a modest registration level of 50-60 percent capacity? Is the amount of money you will take home at 50-60 percent capacity an exciting amount of revenue for you to earn for the amount of time that will go into preparing for, marketing, and leading the event? If not, take a look at some of the variables you can adjust to make the financial scenario more favorable:

How would a small increase or decrease to the ticket price affect the total program net revenue? ____________________

____

How would a small increase or decrease in the revenue share or percentage split change your total take-home pay? ____________________

____

What other observations can you make about the relationship between your event's expenses, capacity for revenue, and your take-home pay? ____________________

____

____

It is a great practice to run the numbers, and then run them again on every single event that you consider participating in before you say yes. It will help you create better financial outcomes for yourself and keep you from learning certain mistakes the hard way.

Available online on HK*Propel*.

Learning From My Own Mistakes

In 2014, Sadie and I hosted a yoga and wine retreat in the gorgeous hills of Tuscany, in central Italy. We both lived in Brooklyn and had befriended a wonderful man, Don, who owned a gorgeous bed and breakfast called At Home in Brooklyn. He was a fabulous home chef and a food and wine connoisseur. Don had lived in Tuscany for many years after he'd retired from Wall Street and said that he knew Tuscany "like the back of my hand." Over a few glasses of wine (work your network, people!), we decided that because we all loved wine and yoga and Sadie was Italian, why not partner on creating fabulous yoga and wine events in Tuscany?

Neither Sadie, Don, nor I had ever led a retreat before, but we knew we had students who were madly in love with Sadie and were ready to make an investment in time and money to travel with us, and Don certainly knew Tuscany. Don was responsible for all the logistics on the ground: arranging the transfers and buses, booking the restaurants and excursions, planning the meals, and reserving the yoga spaces and guest lodging in the charming town of Montalcino.

Meanwhile, Sadie and I were responsible for marketing, registration, and taking care of the guests from the time they inquired about the retreat to the time they got home safely. Because we were in charge of registration, we also collected the funds. This was in the early days of e-commerce, so we had multiple streams of incoming money and tons of outgoing expenses being handled in cash by Don in mom-and-pop establishments across Tuscany, all while the currency was fluctuating—and not in our favor.

We sold out the entire retreat in less than a month, and we were flying high! Time to raise a glass and bring on la dolce vita, y'all! The retreat was a huge success, and everyone had a truly amazing time. I still look at the photos and pinch myself, thinking, "Did we really live in a medieval village for a week and do yoga in the vineyards of Tuscany?" We sure did!

© Alessandro Moggi

Yoga retreat in Italy, as the sun was setting on the island of Salina. This pose, for me, *is* the yoga business: rooted and stable in where we've come from, while gazing forward and reaching boldly into the future.

(continued)

Learning From My Own Mistakes *(continued)*

When we got home to settle up finances for the retreat, we were all in for quite a shock. Not only did our oh-so-fabulous wine and yoga retreat not make a profit, but we actually ended up owing quite a bit of money. Not exactly the happiest of endings, and this not-so-happy ending is unfortunately common.

We made a few huge mistakes. We priced the retreat according to what we *thought* was a good price: a decent markup on what we *thought* our expenses would be, which ended up being a double whammy. Because we weren't properly tracking expenses in relation to the price, not only did we miscalculate what we spent, but we also miscalculated what we made—if we calculated anything properly at all!

These miscalculations may seem naive, but this happens regularly when planning a large-format program. It can be difficult to get all of the details in one place at one time (fixed costs) and to properly anticipate what might not work out the way you think it will (e.g., low registration) or anticipate the things that you cannot see that will affect the bottom line (e.g., fluctuations in currency exchange rates). The result is underestimating the real costs and responsibilities of an event. Even the simple addition of a contingency fee of $50 to $100 per person to pad your budget for the unexpected or including the 3.5 percent credit card fee per transaction can make an enormous difference to your bottom line. If you collect fees in dollars and spend them in euros, monies will be lost on the exchange.

The list of variables is long, which is why using an event calculator is necessary when executing trainings, immersions, and retreats, and so is learning from other people's mistakes! Trust me: You don't want to learn these things on your own, and you certainly don't need to learn everything the hard way.

We have now reviewed all of the yoga services, including business types and service models. It's so exciting to see in one place all of the individual components that you can use to build your yoga business! In chapter 7, we will look at how you can use the Internet to deliver your yoga services by learning how to run and operate a virtual yoga studio. The Internet is an entirely new marketplace for your business!

7 VIRTUAL OFFERINGS

I would guess that before the pandemic, 80 percent of yoga teachers were not teaching yoga online, and many yoga teachers were vehemently opposed to doing so. The reasons they were opposed were many: It isn't real yoga if it's online. It's impossible to have genuine connection with students online. It's impossible for students to retain information they gain online.

The pandemic accelerated the adoption and implementation of many technologies that would have taken years, if not decades, to become mainstream (Elnaj 2021). Many of the pre-COVID-19 naysayers have found that they actually love to teach online, their students respond and absorb content exceptionally well in the online environment, and they recognize that teaching online allows them to expand their classroom's reach worldwide. In addition, licensing bodies such as the Yoga Alliance have allowed for accreditation online, revolutionizing the way that longer-format yoga experiences are delivered.

This is the Zoom boom, a new era of teaching and learning yoga that emerged out of necessity and is definitely here to stay.

So, like it or not, this is the Zoom boom, a new era of teaching and learning yoga that emerged out of necessity and is definitely here to stay. (I am not so sure about those pandemic sweat suits, though.) If you haven't gotten fully into the online game, don't worry; it is not too late. If you have an active student base or are building one, simply consider your online studio as an additional location where you will teach them and start building there, too. The cat is out of the bag when it comes to practicing, teaching, and living yoga online, and as the world emerges from the pandemic, the online studio space will continue to be increasingly commonplace and vital to our industry.

As a student, I have taken my fair share of online yoga classes and trainings, and as a teacher, I have also led my fair share of online yoga classes and trainings. It has been quite a learning curve, especially considering the speed with which we were forced to migrate online. But we made it. A lot of lessons have been learned, a lot of bloopers have been made, and I've narrowed them down to a chapter containing the best of the best practices for creating a great virtual classroom.

Real Talk

"Teaching virtually has allowed me to reach people from all over the world; my online course has reached 162 countries. That would never happen in a live format. Online, there's no limit. So I've been able to make, frankly, more money with less effort—but I really miss the human contact."
Anodea Judith
Author, public speaker, and therapist

TOOLS AND EQUIPMENT

One of the things I love the most about yoga is that you don't need tools or equipment to practice it, other than yourself and your breath. However, having a good set of tools and equipment in your virtual classroom is vital to facilitating quality delivery and an easeful experience for both you and your students. Let's take a peek at some of the tools and equipment that I have used to accomplish just that.

Software

There are many platforms for setting up a virtual classroom. Zoom Pro is the most ubiquitous, and for a good reason—it is really simple to use. It isn't called the Zoom boom for nothing! Keep simplicity in mind when choosing software because complicated software can be paralyzing. Start with something simple and add complexity later as your online needs grow. Other great options for virtual classrooms include Union, Ribbon, and Namastream. The platforms we love for large-format online learning include Teachable, Thinkific, and Kajabi. Make sure that your choice of platform integrates with your payment portals and bookkeeping system so you have the reporting you need at the end of the year to file your taxes.

Hardware

Create a high-quality virtual classroom experience by investing in high-quality equipment. High quality does not mean expensive; this means committing to the fact that you are running an online yoga studio and making sure that you have the right and necessary components to do so. It took me almost a year before I decided I needed to get an LED light, create a backdrop for myself, and quit running around five minutes before every Zoom session looking for a place to prop up my smartphone, which would inevitably tip over one minute before the event was about to begin. It was completely and unnecessarily stressful to be that unprepared and an illustration of my denial that the virtual classroom was the reality of my day-to-day yoga business.

Real Talk

"Invest in good equipment."
Dharma Mittra
Yoga teacher, practitioner, and guru of modern yoga

So what is the right and necessary equipment? Here's what I suggest:

- *Tripod*: I love a sturdy and adjustable tripod that allows you to record from different angles and different heights.
- *Microphone*: I suggest the RODE Wireless GO for video production and wireless earbuds with ear hooks for Zoom Pro and live teaching.
- *Light source*: Natural light is best. Use LED when natural light is not possible, and try to always light from behind your camera.
- *Reliable Internet connection*: Like seriously—really, really good. Being dropped from your session creates stress for you and dissatisfaction for your clients.
- *Charging cable*: Don't be *that* teacher whose battery dies while they are in the middle of teaching online! It really can happen so make sure you have plenty of charging cables.

PRODUCTION BEST PRACTICES

Create an amazing community vibe online to keep your students coming back for more.

Now that your virtual studio is equipped, let's get into how to produce an optimal virtual classroom experience for yourself and the students. The production best practices include tips on how to use your tools and equipment well; how to prepare yourself and the virtual classroom; how to support students administratively as they enter, practice, and exit; and fun ways to create an amazing community vibe and keep your students coming back for more.

Consider the angles.

While you are doing your walkthrough and testing the placement of your equipment, consider how you can be seen from different angles in the frame. Most teachers show their entire body on the mat during an online event, which can often take them quite far from the camera. Don't be afraid during the cuing of the class or as you lecture to get closer to your virtual students by talking directly into the camera. The closer you are, the more you can make eye contact, which will increase connection and engagement in your productions.

Try a two-camera setup.

Camera one can be logged in as the host and camera two as the cohost. This allows you to watch your classes on both speaker view and gallery view at the same time *and* to record in two camera positions at the same time. It also allows you to have a backup camera running in case one of your cameras goes down.

Film horizontally.

When you are setting up your virtual studio, make sure that your camera device is turned to its horizontal, or landscape, format. The majority of platforms where your classes will be uploaded need the classes recorded in horizontal format.

Create a clean visual experience.

Teaching yoga online means that for most of us, our home becomes the yoga studio—both for teachers and students. Pay particular attention to making your online yoga studio awesome, as if those students were walking into your very own home for the first time. Your cat crawling into your practice space is cute, but seeing your dirty dishes and your dirty laundry is not. Remember that you are still a leader and in a position of power—even when in the comfort of your own home. When someone can see into your home, it creates a sense of intimacy, which is both good and bad. Setting a professional tone and boundary from a visual point of view is important. The cleaner and more professional your space looks, the better you will be able to keep boundaries and the more professionally you can run your business overall.

Do a walk-through.

I love to do a walk-through rehearsal in my virtual classroom before leading or recording so I can anticipate my and the students' experience. A walk-through allows you to experience the event in the virtual classroom in real life and to live what the event feels like each step of the way: the log-in or entry experience, the waiting room or preshow experience, the in-class experience or main event, and the exit after the event concludes or the postshow. Experiencing what your students experience gives you a chance to look for moments in which you can improve or enhance the overall encounter. The walk-through also allows you to set up and test your hardware in advance. You can even mark the floor with tape where your camera tripod and your yoga mat need to be placed for the perfect frame.

Start on time.

If you are late to an in-person program, students can connect with each other and keep themselves occupied while they wait for you to arrive and for class to begin. I have fond memories of the anticipation of waiting in a packed classroom on my yoga mat for a teacher who was a few minutes late to arrive. However, when you're teaching in a virtual classroom and you are late, there's nothing happening for the participants other than waiting for you to show up. This is why it is important to start your online events on time or have someone there early to host and welcome people for you. We will talk more about this later.

ADMINISTRATIVE SUPPORT

The business practices you use for your virtual classroom should be the same as you use for your in-person studio. You want a smooth, seamless experience from the time someone learns about your online classes via your marketing, to the moment they register for class in the virtual studio, to the moment they log out. The goal is for the online process to be thorough and thoughtful, as if you were welcoming someone into your own home. So let's look at administrative considerations that will help you to create a thoughtful and thorough experience.

Provide tech support.

It is a big task to manage both hosting and teaching in a virtual classroom. Many savvy teachers have an assistant who is the host or moderator of the event. Think of that person as a producer who is responsible for greeting the students and providing tech support. This is similar to how front desk staff at an actual studio greet and support students. Students are tolerant of technical difficulties, but that doesn't mean that you as the teacher preparing to deliver an exceptional class need to be the one fixing them. That time could be spent engaging and building community with your students.

Set prices and packages.

When migration to the virtual classroom began, we weren't sure the same pricing model used for an in-person studio was appropriate. We wondered whether we should lower the price for online events. (If you recall, many of us thought initially that the virtual classroom was a less-than experience.) We quickly learned that online events were similar to in-person events and that the prices should be similar as well. In addition to using a similar per-class pricing structure, you can package your virtual studio offerings using the same methodology as your in-person offering. In chapter 8, we will dive deep into pricing and packaging!

Conduct a thorough student registration.

Also similar to what they use in an in-person studio, a savvy virtual studio owner will re-create a thorough student registration process for collecting contact information, obtaining waivers of liability, and distributing new-student information. Having the basic contact details for students in your virtual classes is important for both future marketing needs and operations. Having the students sign waivers of liability confirms

Use new-student information to create a world-class experience for your students by personally orienting and welcoming them into your virtual studio.

that they know what they are getting themselves into and that they are the ones responsible for their health in the virtual classroom. You can find sample waivers online, and I suggest paying a lawyer for an hour of time to review your waiver and make sure that your online studio is protected.

Use new-student information to create a world-class experience for your students by personally orienting and welcoming them into your virtual studio. If a new student entered a physical space, you would welcome them, show them where the bathrooms are, and where to grab a tea and store their things. You would also share with them the culture of the studio—who you are and what you stand for—and set mutual behavioral expectations. You would also share housekeeping rules such as whether or not cameras or recording in class is allowed. What you want to do is mimic the new-student experience in your virtual classroom as if your student were walking into a physical space.

Provide your policies.

Make sure that all of the policies and the policies with penalties related to lateness, cancellations, and expiration dates discussed in chapter 5 are present in your virtual studio. This can be accomplished through a separate page on your website that lists your policies and an opt-in statement; at the time of registration, students must confirm by ticking a box that they have read the policies for your virtual studio.

Respect copyright.

Don't use images, videos, or music if you don't have the rights to them. There are lots of free image options out there; keep your content and the use of other

FatCamera/E+/Getty Images

Whether you're offering one-to-one training, group sessions, or large-format online events, the virtual classroom is viable and here to stay! Have fun, and make the most of it.

Your Yoga Business Homework

Take Your Own Virtual Class

Now that you have learned best practices for your virtual studio, let's put your current setup to the test by taking your own recorded virtual class. Although many people dislike looking at themselves talking on camera, what better way to receive feedback and improve your production and delivery than actually taking your own recorded class? (The whole thing, take the entire class!) This will allow you to be in the seat of the student and to truly understand what their experience taking your class is like.

After taking your own yoga class online, complete the following questions:

What was my registration process like? ______________________________

____

Does the class look good? ______________________________

____

Does it sound good? ______________________________

____

Is my instruction easy to follow? ______________________________

____

How does the online class feel? ______________________________

____

Have I created a welcoming atmosphere in the online environment? _____

____

____

Is my personality coming across the way that it would in a physical space? _____

____

____

Am I interacting consistently with the students, whether by giving verbal adjustments or positive feedback? ______________________________

____

What do I love about my virtual event? ______________________________

____

What else can I do to improve or enhance my virtual class experience? _________

____

people's materials above board. Some teachers even make playlists separately on a music-streaming platform like Spotify to go alongside their classes to completely separate the music from the class itself.

Create community.

Just because you can't congregate physically in person before and after class doesn't mean that you can't create a community intentionally in your online studio environment. Think about ways you can get to know your students and help the students get to know each other within the virtual environment. Community building is a great opportunity to engage with your students and to keep them coming back for more. Ways to create community include making sure the students' Zoom profiles list the names they would like to be called and their pronouns, too. You can also have the waiting room open for a few minutes before class begins to let people chat and mingle with each other, and you can stay in the room after class ends to answer questions and make small talk before hopping off of the Zoom session. These are all great ways to create community online.

Teach live regularly.

Students love new content. You will have much greater demand for your live online classes and events than you will for recordings and playbacks. There is just something better about today's Saturday class than last week's Saturday class. Keep the schedule of your live online classes consistent and teach as often as is sustainable for you to do so to give your students many options when they can log in and practice live. It creates regularity, excitement, and anticipation when your students know there is something new to look forward to. These are important factors for keeping your students coming back.

ADDITIONAL CONSIDERATIONS FOR ONLINE LARGE-FORMAT PROGRAMS

As we covered in chapter 6, workshops, trainings, immersions, and retreats are large-format programs that can be offered live or by recording in a virtual classroom in addition to in person. You may wish to create an online course such as a recorded workshop or training that students can access when it's convenient for them. Because of the amount of online time required for your students to partake in these large-format virtual programs, it is important to make concessions.

Consider Zoom fatigue.

Zoom fatigue is real. Now that I work from home and online most weeks, I find that come Thursday, my eyes are tired, and I have a shorter attention span after three days of looking at the screen. Your students get bored and get tired too. Being online for long durations is different from when they were in the room with you. Even the most engaging yoga teacher can become a talking robot, and even the most well-intended student can hit the wall and become blank screens. To combat Zoom fatigue, encourage students to keep their cameras on (it is not legal to enforce it); regularly intersperse lectures with movement, conversation, or debate; and most importantly, check in for feedback throughout the program by asking the students how they are doing and adjusting as needed. Be prepared and willing to be flexible with the teaching schedule in order to meet both your and your students' needs.

Your Yoga Business Homework

Take a Training, or Invite a Guest

Being the teacher of a large-format program is a lot different from being the student. Put yourself in the students' shoes and take a full day of someone else's program and invite them to take a day of yours. Perhaps this is another teacher you are friends with and are comfortable exchanging honest critiques with. This exercise is a great way to receive feedback from a peer that will improve the production, process, and delivery in your large-format programs.

Available online on HK*Propel*.

Make the learning manageable.

When you're teaching online, you need to teach in smaller, bite-sized chunks than you would in an in-person environment. Keep it simple, focus on one thing at a time, and take breaks often. Consider at each step of the way how to measure the effectiveness of the program. How will you know if the students get it? What do you want students to be able to do or understand as a result of your large-format training? Can you build in ways to assess their comprehension each step of the way?

Make the content applicable.

Consider how your students can practice in real life what they're learning online. How can you create opportunities for students to integrate and apply what they have learned rather than just simply watch a lecture? How can they take it into the real world and implement it right away? Create opportunities for conversation and debate among students in your large-format programs and incorporate real-world exercises. These strategies will help students to apply the content.

Repurpose your resources.

What resources do you have from other programs that can be used within your large-format program? For instance, if your goal is to develop a 12-hour online immersion, why not reuse some of your existing recorded lectures, ebooks or PDFs, slideshows, podcasts, vlogs and blogs, and animations in addition to the new content you will create?

You may not need to create as much new content as you think in order to build a large-format experience, and there is nothing wrong with repurposing. Not only is it efficient to reuse existing materials, but it also allows for much-needed visual variety and learning diversity—which are important to combat Zoom fatigue.

Anticipate no-shows.

Another unique characteristic of the online environment is that students are more impulsive with online purchases than they are with in-person purchases. This means that many students have no intention of completing an online program—some just buy for the sake of buying—so don't be dismayed if students do not complete their program. Despite this reality, build your programs by aiming for the highest completion rate possible; after all, you want your students to experience your teachings and to have the greatest opportunity for results.

Thinking through the following questions will go a long way toward increasing your completion rate:

- How can you keep the students engaged and connected?
- Can they work in groups before and throughout the program to support retention and to create more of a high-touch experience?
- Will you assess comprehension? If so, how?
- When the students reach completion, what do they get (e.g., certificates of completion)? Is this clearly advertised?

To sum up, there are myriad ways to leverage the power of the Internet simply, efficiently, and effectively across your yoga business. Whether for one-to-one sessions or large-format programs, you can create, maintain, and level up your yoga business by harnessing the power of the Internet. We have now covered all yoga services, both in person and online, which means it's time to discuss yoga goods.

8
MENU OF SERVICES

Most yoga teachers would like to make more money; heck, almost everyone would like to make more money. And more often than not, people tend to think about marketing first when thinking about how to earn more money. And that's not wrong—the more people who know about you, the more people there are to consume your yoga goods and services. However, getting your name out is only effective if you can sell well-packaged yoga goods and services. And most yoga professionals pay little attention to how they package and sell their goods and services. You might be scratching your head right now, so let me give you an example of what I mean.

Not having properly packaged yoga goods and services is like hearing about an amazing restaurant, deciding to try it, and then finding it difficult to order your meal. When you walk in, you can see and smell all of the delicious food, but no one tells you how to order it or what it will cost. No one tells you how much is served in one portion, if you can come back for more, what to do if you'd like to buy dinner for a friend, whether you can have it delivered, and so on. Having a menu that clearly describes what's offered and the ingredients, substitution options, how much it will cost, payment options, and other available products and services is so important that an entire role within the restaurant industry is dedicated to writing great menus.

The clearer you are about what you offer and how much it costs, the easier it will be for you to sell your goods and services and increase your income.

PRICING AND PACKAGING YOUR SERVICES

The clearer you are about what you offer and how much it costs, the easier it will be for you to sell your goods and services and increase your income. As a matter of fact, I call pricing and packaging your services *a menu of services*. Once you've done the hard work of getting someone interested enough to walk into your business, you have to do your best to make it easy for them to complete a purchase from a menu that is easy to follow.

When I go to a yoga teacher's website, I often cannot easily locate the store or see what they're selling. They might say that they offer private sessions, but then there is no way to purchase a private session, or a pack of them for that matter. I know that many teachers don't want to sell a private session online because they like to interview their potential private clients before saying yes to providing them the service. While this lack of transparency can be intentional, 9 times out of 10, a good or service is hard to find because the yoga professional has not focused on what goods and services to provide, how to describe them, how to price them, and how to make them easy to find on the website. All this makes it difficult to generate revenue in their business. The solution to this problem is a well-thought-out pricing and packaging strategy for the yoga goods and services your business offers and you want to sell more of.

In the same way that a relationship with your main yoga services builds and strengthens gradually—free content leads to group classes, group classes lead to workshops, workshops lead to one-to-ones, and one-to-ones lead to teacher training—pricing and packaging your goods and services should follow a similar pattern.

The first step in learning how to price, package, and prioritize your goods and services is to create your product concepts. Product concepts are groups of goods and services that you sell within your business (we'll learn more about these in detail in the next section). Then, once you have decided what product concepts you will sell, you must also set a price and choose a brand name for each good or service. You will also need to write clear and attractive product descriptions. When done well, they are an excellent way to create brand recognition and excitement in the market (more on that in a minute). Your product description will answer these questions:

- What are you selling? (Describe the type of yoga good or service.)
- What problems are you solving for your clients? (Clearly describe the need or want that your client has and how this addresses it.)
- What does the client get for the price they are paying? (Be as explicit as possible when listing what the clients receive.)

UNDERSTANDING PRODUCT CONCEPTS

Product concepts are groups of goods and services that you sell within your business. In the next section, I will provide a sample menu of services that will include product descriptions, pricing, and brand names, but let's first take a closer look at the product concepts—trial sessions or sample offerings, single and package sessions, loyalty packages, and premium products or signature offers. These are vital to your business as is the pricing strategy that goes with each.

Trial Sessions or Sample Offerings

One of the most overlooked and important elements of a complete menu of services is a trial session or sample offering. This allows a potential client to sample the service before committing to buying. Granny used to say, "No one is going to buy a cow if they haven't tasted the milk yet," and a savvy yoga professional will offer a free 15-minute consultation or regularly host a free program that allows potential clients to sample the wares. This doesn't need to be a huge free offering, and it can be offered on a limited basis, but I recommend having a way to serve your potential clients that is not behind a paywall. Many teachers who want to sell more charge for 100 percent of their products. You may feel that you are standing for your worth by not working for free, but you are also creating a bottleneck in your business. The reality is that it takes a tremendous amount of trust for someone to work with you, and while many people are enthusiastic about you and your business, they need reassurance to complete their purchase and commit to working with you, especially for your goods and services with higher time commitments and prices.

Trust and credibility in your business are assets that grow over time as you continue to deliver a solid product. When you have developed enough trust and credibility, you may be able to eliminate the trial session or sample offering, as I have after more than 10 years in business. I still do a trial consultation, but it is no longer free. I still regularly hold free programs (often underwritten by another company so I still get paid) where I can spend time with interested clients who are considering whether my services are a good fit.

If you choose to charge for your trial session or sample offering, the price should not be a barrier to entry by causing an interested client a moment's hesitation in purchasing the trial—not a moment. Every teacher's client base is different, so I cannot say what your ideal trial session or sample price should be, although I often arrive at this price by working backward from the price of the single session.

Single and Package Sessions

A single-session rate can range from $49 to $499. Yes, the range is that wide. Here are the factors that play into setting your single-session rate:

- *The market in which you live*—Are you in a big city or a country with a higher-valued currency? Do you live in a town with an established yoga market with a lot of yoga businesses, or are you creating the market?
- *Your level of experience*—How long have you been teaching and how experienced are you? People pay more for experience.
- *The strength of your reputation*—Do you have a wealth of testimonials from happy or important clients? People pay more for credibility.
- *Buzz*—Have you recently received a public acknowledgment or upgraded your business? Are folks talking about you? A time when your business has buzz is a great time to adjust your rate.
- *Reality*—What does it cost you to deliver the service? Yoga professionals often forget to calculate prep time, travel time, and wait time (in addition to delivery time of the service) when considering where to set a single-session price. Keep this additional time in mind when setting your price, because often an hour session actually takes two and a half hours of your time.

The goal of clarifying the single-session price is to clearly understand the value of your time. You can pay attention to the prices that your peers charge for a similar good or service, although I encourage my clients to set prices according to their business expenses and revenue goals rather than feeling beholden to what others around them might be doing. Your peers do not have the same experience, reputation, buzz, or expenses that you do, so why would their prices be the same as yours?

The more attentive you are to your business, the market, and fluctuations in demand for your goods and services, the more you will see your pricing as a dial you can adjust and manipulate to serve the moment.

Once you choose your single-session price, you can then price out the rest of your goods and services. Try not to become paralyzed with fear when pricing your yoga goods and services, because price is a flexible component of your business. The more attentive you are to your business, the market, and fluctuations in demand for your goods and services, the more you will see your pricing as a dial you can adjust and manipulate to serve the moment.

If you will offer one-to-one sessions, whether they be mentorship, coaching, or nutrition consultations, there should be options for single sessions and packages of different quantities, such as 4 or 10, to be used by a specific date. As we discussed in chapter 5, packages should have expiration dates. Your rationale for the pricing of single sessions and packages should be incentive based. For example, if your single session rate is $99, then a four pack could be 15 percent less than $396 ($99 × 4). By pricing the four pack at $337, you have given an incentive to the client to purchase it. You can take this logic through the rest of your yoga services. Yes, of course, you want to sell the client on the benefits of committing to their well-being as a strategy to sell a package, but a good price break helps to upsell. Your business will benefit greatly from repeat clients, so selling packages is important to your business.

Offering great packages in your yoga business keeps your clients engaged and coming back for more.

Loyalty Packages

Similar to an annual membership at a yoga studio, a loyalty product allows your most loyal clients to stock up on sessions while providing a fairly steep discount as a reward for their commitment up front. Loyalty packages are often provided as large packages of sessions, unlimited sessions, or long-term contracts, such as annual and semiannual memberships. You may also be able to bundle in additional benefits such as discounts off your other yoga services—workshops, immersions, teacher training—as a way to add value and incentives.

Premium Products or Signature Offers

Your premium product, which is also commonly referred to as a signature offer in business circles, is the most exclusive and expensive product on your menu, a rare and delicious delicacy, as it were. These products are aspirational for your client and potentially game changing for you. I find it interesting that premium doesn't mean big; it means extra. Therefore, a premium product is one that is considered extra special that someone pays an extra price for.

Many yoga businesses do not offer a premium product, which I believe is because yoga professionals find it difficult to accept being paid and being paid what they are worth, let alone being paid a premium for their services. The easiest way to think about a premium product is to think about a designer label. Why would someone pay a premium price of $250 for a brown leather belt when they could get the same leather belt without the label for $25? Because that label stands for something extra special that is associated with quality and a certain *je ne sais quoi* (undefinable characteristic that makes something distinctive). Maybe that certain je ne sais quoi is you. You most likely won't sell a lot of premium products, but it is worthwhile to look at how selling even just a few per year changes your bottom line. It is also interesting to start stretching how much you *think* you are worth by putting prices on the menu that are thought starters—both for you and your client. I mean, what *if* someone paid you *that* much money to teach them yoga?

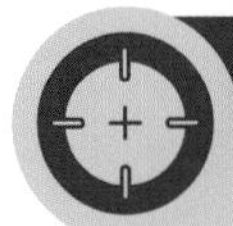

Your Yoga Business Homework

Examine Your Products

Now that you've learned about the main types of products, let's take a look at your current products and start to think about those you can offer in the future by answering these questions:

- Which product concepts are you already using, and what improvements can you make to your existing product concepts?
- Do your product concepts properly explain what you are selling (the type of yoga good or service)?
- What problems do your product concepts solve for your clients (clearly addressing the need or want that your client has)?
- What does the client actually get for the price that they are paying?
- Which new product concepts would you like to use, or do you dream about using?

Based on what you've learned, what kinds of products and brand names can you imagine for your business? Provide ideas for each type here:

Trial sessions or sample offerings: ____________________

____

____

____

Single or package sessions: ____________________

____

____

____

Loyalty packages: ____________________

____

____

____

Premium products or signature offers: ____________________

____

____

____

SAMPLE MENU OF SERVICES

Each of the yoga services you sell becomes part of your menu of services. They coexist, affect, and relate to each other. There should be a natural progression in terms of time commitment, access, and price. I almost never sell a loyalty package or premium product before someone has purchased a few single sessions or a package of sessions. For my clientele, it's just too big a purchase to make without a trial session first.

So, now that we've covered the basics, let's take a look at how I bring the products to life in my actual business. Following is a sample menu of services, along with product descriptions, brand names, and prices. This may help you envision how you could create your own menu of services based on your dream goals.

Sample Trial Sessions or Sample Offerings

Practice Your Yoga Business – $19

To have a great yoga career, you have to spend as much time working on being a great business owner as you do on learning to be a great yoga teacher. Yep, I said it! Working on your business requires commitment and dedication—just like working on your yoga practice. This is why I created Practice Your Business, a 60-minute monthly workshop designed to take your business to the next level. We'll cover the most popular topics from The Catalyst online business school such as identifying your purpose and acting like a boss. Each session includes time for live Q&A.

Starting Gate – $79

Yoga was never intended to be one size fits all, and neither is your yoga business. In this 40-minute "first date" services overview, we dive quickly into what you're looking for and the custom services that we offer. If you think we're a fit but aren't quite sure, the starting gate is the right product for you.

Sample Single and Package Sessions

Assessment (Single Session) – $199

Is it time to take stock of your existing business and to redirect the path that your yoga business is on? Do you need to think in fresh and innovative ways in order to move your business forward or keep your business afloat in the current market environment? Together, we will strategically assess what your business consists of and the direction your business is headed and create a punch list of action steps that are just right for you based on your unique purpose, environment, and opportunities. This session will give you the direction you need to take your business further and faster in the smartest way possible. Tap into over 15 years of experience in negotiating, vetting, and creating opportunities (see our Who We Work For page) as well as launching, maintaining, and leveling up your yoga businesses.

We begin the assessment process by having you complete our signature business analysis module: Own Where You Are to Get Where You Want to Be. Your analysis module is then reviewed before a powerful 90-minute advising session with our founder, Ava Taylor, who will work with you to create your unique punch list of level-up action steps. Create practical and immediate strategies to catalyze your yoga business's growth with our signature assessment.

Gift Certificate (Single Session) – $199

Being an entrepreneur isn't easy. Give the gift of clarity and peace of mind to the yoga entrepreneur in your life with a YAMA Talent gift card. Your loved one is a click away from taking the first step toward becoming their dream. Gift cards are delivered by email and contain instructions for redeeming them at checkout. Our gift cards have no additional processing fees, and we can add a personalized gift note.

Online Business School – $199

The Catalyst online business school delivers the very best of what we've learned in over 10 years working with household name yoga teachers, studios, and brands and with regional rock stars and rookies worldwide. We'll share all the goals, all the wins, all the learnings, all the corrections, and all the common yogi pitfalls.

This isn't everything there is to know about running a yoga business—this is everything that matters. These learnings are distilled into 30 lectures with customizable handouts, resource pages, homework, interactive worksheets, and the tools and templates we use every day to support our clients at YAMA. This premium content covers the areas of analysis, branding, customization, marketing, and execution. The Catalyst was created for the same reasons as YAMA: to advocate for and empower yoga teachers in a market that is moving and changing quickly in order to make it possible to make a living while teaching yoga, and, in doing so, to bring the tools of wellness to communities of all kinds.

The Catalyst is for yogis at all stages of their careers who are looking to take their yoga businesses further, faster. Equip yourself with the tools, knowledge, and know-how you need to catalyze real and sustainable growth as a yoga teacher. Granny always used to say, "If you knew better, you'd do better." And, if you didn't know before, you know now. Welcome to The Catalyst.

Catalyst for Success In-Person Retreat at Kripalu – $350

Equip yourself with the tools and know-how you need to catalyze real and sustainable growth in the healing arts with author, entrepreneur, and small-business coach Ava Taylor. There are myriad opportunities for healing arts practitioners at all stages of their careers to bolster their businesses and to feel empowered doing so. Become proactive, set goals, and regain your motivation to create your next normal. In this interactive, experiential weekend retreat based on Ava's online business school, The Catalyst, and new book, *Your Yoga Business*, you will learn the following:

- How to assess and maximize your existing business
- Methods to regain stability and control of your work
- The latest trends in the market and shifts in consumer behavior
- Ways to make your failures work for you
- Techniques to sell with confidence and to feel empowered moving forward

Create more opportunities for yourself and return home with an actionable 12-month business plan, detailed product menu, and marketing schedule.

Road Map (Four Sessions) – $699

Maximize your existing business and create a powerful and achievable business plan to take your business further, faster. Is it time to take stock of your existing business and to reIMAGINE the path that your yoga business is on? Do you need to think in fresh and innovative ways based on the current market environment in order to move your business forward or keep your business afloat?

If so, the Road Map is for you. Together over the course of four 90-minute sessions, we will strategically assess what your business is composed of and how to maximize what is already there, reIMAGINE the direction your business is headed, and create an in-depth plan of action with detailed strategies to actually get you from where you are to where you want to be. This is your 12-month Career Road Map.

Our four 90-minute sessions are organized as follows (the best pace for this process is one session every other week):

- *Session 1*: Assess and maximize your existing business.
- *Session 2*: reIMAGINE the business of your dreams.
- *Session 3*: Set goals.
- *Session 4*: Identify strategies to reach your goal.

Sample Loyalty Packages

The Finish Line (12 Sessions) – $1,999

We believe having a great team is important in getting stuff done. Get the help and expertise you need to move forward. In this potent one-to-one consulting package, we will tackle multiple high-priority projects that will make a difference to your yoga business and leverage our resources and network to help you quickly make real progress.

The Finish Line Career Coaching Retainer (12 Months) – $1,999

Have pressing business matters? Overwhelmed by emails with invitations to collaborate? Tired of running the race alone? No sounding board to bounce ideas off of, let alone someone to support decision-making and bringing projects to fruition? Achieving substantial growth requires long-term planning and step-by-step guidance and support. An ongoing coaching relationship provides accountability, structure, mentorship, experience, and access.

Tap into over 15 years of experience negotiating, vetting, and creating opportunities (see our Who We Work For page) as well as launching, maintaining, and leveling up yoga businesses. Make sure you are not missing out on things, and make sure you are making the most of things.

In a fast-moving and unpredictable marketplace, nothing creates true progress like having an expert guide who knows you and your business and who is by your side every step of the way. This retainer meets monthly for 12 months.

Sample Premium Products or Signature Offers

Management Unlimited – $9,999

Have pressing business matters? Overwhelmed by emails with invitations to collaborate? Tired of running the race alone? No sounding board to bounce ideas off of, let alone someone to support decision-making and bringing projects to fruition? Achieving substantial growth requires long-term planning and step-by-step guidance and support. An ongoing coaching relationship provides accountability, structure, mentorship, experience, and access.

Tap into over 15 years of experience negotiating, vetting, and creating opportunities (see our Who We Work For page) as well as launching, maintaining, and leveling up yoga businesses. Make sure you are not missing out on things, and make sure you are making the most of things. With the Management Unlimited package, you will receive a year's worth of unlimited coaching sessions, calls, emails, and texts as well as complimentary admission to the Catalyst for Success in-person retreat at Kripalu. This includes annual membership to Practice Your Yoga Business and includes the Road Map, the Accelerator, and The Catalyst online business school for yogis.

As you can see from my menu of services, I've had a lot of fun creating brand names for my products. Keeping in line with the main tagline of the company, Catalyst for Better Living, I chose to create brand names that take into account the motion that a catalyst creates. This is why I call my trial, or sample, session the Starting Gate, the business plan product a Road Map, and the loyalty packages the Finish Line. I want to continue to reinforce to my clients that my goods and services will help them move closer to fulfilling their business dreams.

9
PRODUCTS AND MERCHANDISE

In an industry like yoga, the majority of the time, yoga teachers sell services. In this chapter, we will look at all of the yoga goods—the products and merchandise, both those that you create and those that other companies create—that you can add to your yoga business. We will also look at the types of product deals that can exist between you and those companies. We will look at tips, tools, and best practices for choosing how (or whether) to include yoga goods in your yoga business.

Thinking about selling products and merchandise feels strange to a lot of yoga professionals who aren't used to thinking of themselves as business owners. It is a newer type of yoga service model and the one they have the least amount of experience with. Yoga teachers can convince themselves that they aren't running a business when they're selling their time, but when they're selling T-shirts, it's a little harder to avoid the truth.

Before the Internet and social media, getting a product deal with a company was rare, and producing and selling merchandise was time consuming and expensive. In fact, when I started working with adidas in 2010, they were the first major non-yoga company to endorse a yoga teacher as a professional athlete with a formal, multiyear contract. Before this historic product deal, only yoga companies like Gaiam offered product deals to a handful of yoga teachers each year to create products such as DVDs. Other than that, few companies across all industries were interested in yoga teachers. In the years since, YAMA has made product deals with major companies who sell yoga content and apparel such as Athleta, lululemon, Nike, The Gap, Under Armour, and Beachbody and to non-yoga companies such as Aetna, Hanes, Kashi, H&M, Minute Maid, Nubian Heritage, Urban Outfitters, and many more. In fact, with the emergence of social media and the ability of individuals to build substantial followings of people, the number and variety of product deals has exploded as companies try to leverage the reach of influencers.

It's been a wild ride since those early days as companies have finally begun to financially value the relationship between themselves, the market, and the yoga teacher. Gone are the days when the expectation was for a yoga teacher to market a product for free. Also gone are the days when one had to buy blank goods, manually imprint them, and sell them out of the trunk of a car or from a living room—the way that most artists used to handle the production and distribution of their merchandise. The Internet now makes it easier to find opportunities to create merchandise quickly and inexpensively.

I hope you'll welcome the opportunity to build your business using this exciting service model. Let's take a closer look at the types of product deals available and the ways you can sell your products and merchandise.

UNDERSTANDING THE TYPES OF PRODUCT DEALS

With product deals everywhere, it's important to improve your knowledge in this area. A savvy teacher knows how to gauge their market value, how to vet and negotiate opportunities, how to interact with product companies, and how to generate more product opportunities for their business. Here are the types of product deals in the market and the nature of each of these relationships.

Endorsement or Spokesperson Deals

These are typically national or international relationships in which you are paid for associating with a company. They use your name, image, and likeness to sell their products across their sales channels and points of contact and across yours. These are typically exclusive relationships (meaning you cannot work at the same time with competitors of the company) and have limited terms of one to three years. I highly recommend having your endorsement deal or spokesperson deal negotiated by an agent or a lawyer. These opportunities are limited, and in order to be considered for one of these opportunities, yoga teachers have to match specific criteria in terms of physical appearance, physical ability, size of their reach, and their yoga specialty or niche.

Endorsement or spokesperson deals align with the company's larger marketing strategy and plans, which change often; what and who are desired by the company today may not be their goal tomorrow. Because these marketing strategies are fickle, I consider these types of product deals as *nice to have, but not need to have*. I prefer for my clients to focus on the controllable elements of their yoga business like setting great goals and making sure that their service model and menu of services are strong. We may say yes to a product deal that comes our way, and we may on occasion seek out product deals, but product deals are not a required element of success.

Activities that are part of endorsement and spokesperson deals may include teaching or public speaking at live appearances, including in front of the media and at press conferences. Activities can include modeling (where the images will be used varies by contract—for example, in-store signage, billboards, websites) and appearing in social media campaigns. These deals also typically offer access to lots of free products.

In addition to the companies listed earlier, companies such as Foot Locker and Reebok as well as brands such as Aquaphor, smartwater, Tom's of Maine, and Weleda offer endorsement deals.

Brand Ambassadorships

These are typically local or regional relationships in which you may not be monetarily compensated for associating with a company and its products. Ambassadorships can be exclusive or nonexclusive, and opportunities are plentiful. The company will use your name, image, likeness, and communication channels to sell their products. Activities within this category include receiving free products or discounts on products, visible placement of the product on your platform and theirs, social media campaigns, and possibly live appearances. Many local and regional companies offer brand ambassadorships as a way to market their products.

Product Trades and Sponsorships

In product trade relationships, you exchange marketing support on your platform for free products from a company. You may offer to run a social media campaign for the company or to sample their products at your live events. Depending on the value of the products, these can be highly lucrative relationships even though no money is exchanged. For instance, many yoga teachers travel to exotic locations on product trades and post on their social media in exchange for a free stay. Sometimes a product trade relationship is called an ambassadorship.

Sponsorship typically refers to a company paying you money to represent their products at an in-person or online event; this guarantees visibility to consumers. I have had single-day events for 25 people sponsored and had multicity international tours for 10,000 people sponsored. Getting products in front of consumers is important to companies, so events of any size are eligible. But be wary: Securing sponsorship takes a lot of work because most sponsorship deals are set in coordination with marketing plans six months to a year before an event.

Affiliate Deals

In these national or international relationships, you receive a percentage of each sale of the company's product that you market to your audience. The sales are tracked via unique links and codes that credit you as the source of a sale, even if someone clicks from your website to the product's website weeks later. Affiliate product deals are nonexclusive and plentiful because almost all companies employ some kind of affiliate strategy.

As yoga continues to increase in popularity, the overall size of the market will also continue to grow. This means that the yoga teacher is at the center point between

Your Yoga Business Homework

List Your Favorite Products

Make a list of the products you use often and love and would be honored to share with your followers. As you make your list, be sure to include local and regional companies and products as well as household name companies. There are many opportunities to collaborate within a two-mile (3.2 km) radius of your home or home studio. Do not underestimate the power of local, especially for my hometown heroes and regional rock stars out there. There is a ton of business to be developed and value added for these local companies. Local relationships can be created and nurtured for a lifetime because you have daily direct access to potential clients. For instance, your favorite local juice bar might be looking for more clients. As a local teacher you are in the perfect position to help them access new health-minded individuals, and your proximity to the juice bar means that the folks you introduce to their products can immediately affect sales. In chapter 17, I will teach you how to pitch and approach your list of favorite brands for product deals.

the products and consumers. This means that the value of the yoga teacher in influencing and driving sales will also continue to grow. I expect to see new types of product deals develop and to see existing deals increase. Now that we've discussed ways you can partner to sell other people's products, let's talk about how to produce and sell products of your own.

SELLING YOUR OWN MERCHANDISE

Merch! I will never forget the blogger who in 2014 literally called YAMA the devil because we suggested that a good way for yoga teachers to diversify their business could be by making a T-shirt with a tagline on it. As far as I am concerned, half the reason to go to your favorite band's concert (or your favorite anywhere) is to get a T-shirt or a tote bag with a tagline on it as a memento. But for one reason or another, this was forbidden in the yoga space for many years. I'm glad to see that the opinions about merchandise have begun to change. I think that if people love you, love the community around you, love your brand, love the practice, and want to rock a piece of merchandise with your logo, your tagline, or even your face on it, then so be it!

Not only has the opinion on yoga merchandise changed, but so has the technology required to create it. Not so long ago you had to buy 1,000 T-shirts at a time to get decent pricing, commit to what you would print on the merchandise well in advance of knowing what the client wanted, and then sell them in person one item at a time. I'm talking about managing suitcases of merchandise, licking stamps, and stuffing envelopes, y'all! Now with the Internet and the ability to print on demand (the merchandise is created when an order is received), you can launch a merchandise shop from a website (see e-commerce on page 141) with little to no up-front cost, and the company that prints the goods can ship the orders to the customers for you. (Although I do know a lot of yoga businesses who still run their merch shops the old-fashioned way!)

YAMA Talent offers a popular line of Y-O-G-A merchandise, including this sweatshirt worn by Dr. Ietef Vita.

Real Talk

"I understand the weight of my words and endorsement. Therefore, if a product was sold, it was sold because I wholeheartedly believed in it...and these offerings helped the bottom line in revenue on a consistent basis. I believe every entrepreneur should find ways to cultivate multiple streams of income that are authentic."
Erica Garcia Abergel
E-RYT 500 yoga teacher, trainer, and continuing education provider

It is smart to think about merchandise from a brand-building perspective. It's been amazing to see boutique fitness studios invest in the merchandise component as a way to build community. There was a time in New York City that you just had to have SoulCycle sweatpants. It wasn't enough that you'd taken class; you needed to represent your studio on the street, too. Nothing says you're part of a community more than proudly wearing the uniform.

My closet has a stack of T-shirts from yoga studios or events that I've practiced at around the world over the past decade. It's a walk down memory lane, and I'm so glad that I have those T-shirts because they are reminders of good times and great moments. I can wear one and reminisce the same way I might pull on a well-worn T-shirt from a concert. If you have never considered creating merchandise, I encourage you to do so. It doesn't need to be big or fancy to be meaningful or to generate revenue. These mementos are also great ways to stay top of mind with a student.

Savvy yoga business owners will look for creative ways to incorporate the sale of products and merchandise across all of their service models. Some even have an e-commerce shop on their website to facilitate the sale of products and merchandise.

In the music world, merchandise accounts for 60 percent of revenue for most artists, and the concert itself is mainly considered an avenue to sell merchandise. If we apply this same thinking to what we have already learned, then your one-to-ones, group sessions, workshops, trainings, immersions, and retreats are also avenues to get customers to the point of purchase for buying merchandise. That's how important products and merchandise can be to overall business health. Savvy yoga business owners will look for creative ways to incorporate the sale of products and merchandise across all of their service models and some even have an e-commerce shop on their website to facilitate the sale of products and merchandise. For example, you can bundle an essential oil and a branded T-shirt into the price of a one-to-one session or use these items as add-ons to increase sales of your large-format programs. I have plenty of clients who ship a box of products and merchandise to a host venue where they are traveling to teach or who carry a suitcase full of products and merchandise with them on the road. The possibilities to create and sell products and merchandise are endless.

Your Yoga Business Homework

Identify Product and Merchandise Ideas

For each of the following service models, make a list of ways you can create opportunities to sell products and merchandise to your students.

One-to-one sessions: ____________________

____

____

Group sessions: ____________________

____

____

Conferences and festivals: ____________________

____

____

Workshops: ____________________

____

____

Immersions: ____________________

____

____

Retreats: ____________________

____

____

Trainings: ____________________

____

Great work, y'all! We have completed parts I and II of *Your Yoga Business*. Our next step in taking your yoga business to the next level is to thoroughly understand your existing yoga business. This will give you the clarity needed to determine what your next level is and set your sights on it. Let's do this!

PART III
BUILD YOUR BUSINESS PLAN

10
ASSESS YOUR EXISTING BUSINESS

Everyone wants to get to their next level, and everyone can—but if you don't know the level you're starting from, it's a heck of a lot harder. This simple truth means that an honest, comprehensive, and granular assessment to uncover precisely where your business is, is crucial to the development of your yoga business. It's like setting the beginning destination when you use a ride-share service like Uber or look for directions on the map app on your smartphone. You cannot choose the best route to a destination without knowing your starting point. This is the same for your business. To get to your next level, you have to establish your starting point. The destination will be the goals you want to reach in your yoga business, and the route you choose to get there will be your business plan. Without knowing point A, you cannot get to point B.

As entrepreneurs with daily duties and urgent issues to tend to, yoga professionals are often too busy running the business day to day to take the time to *pause* and *assess*. They are often too busy putting out fires to identify and track their successes (both monetary and nonmonetary), let alone to spend time thinking about how to capitalize on these successes. They are too busy going from one event to the next to identify and track failures: what they learned, how to resolve the issues, and how to avoid these issues moving forward. They are too busy managing the team to see the growth opportunities sitting right under their noses.

The reduction of busyness caused by the COVID-19 pandemic was a bittersweet silver lining. We were all forced to *pause* and *assess*. The busyness was eliminated or shifted enough to give us an opportunity to gain perspective and to ask ourselves what was working in our businesses and personal lives and what was not. What was most important in each of these areas? Were we acting in alignment with our priorities? This contemplation and assessment is more important now than ever before because there is more opportunity to create now than ever before. For in the upheaval in our yoga industry, we found new possibilities and ways to create. The great pause gave us an incredible chance to assess, reset, recreate, and refine our goals.

Real Talk

"When making important business decisions, it's important to remain flexible, and with the Buddhist mindset that everything is created to be born, to have its journey, to die, and be reborn again, this means that in my business I had to be willing to let go—if you didn't let go, you were going to drown. The biggest lesson was remembering that your yoga is your journey, and it's also a lifelong practice. Letting go allowed me to let the business evolve over time, how it needed to."

Erica Garcia Abergel

E-RYT 500 yoga teacher, trainer, and continuing education provider

I did a lot of one-to-one and group sessions of business support during all phases of the pandemic: as the wave was swelling and we speculated on what its encroachment would mean, as it crested and its true height finally became clear, and when it crashed down on us, mightier and more devastating than any of us expected. I surveyed the damage in awe of how some businesses were devastated entirely and how some were spared, and I watched with bated breath as the effects of the pandemic ebbed and then rose up to come for us again. Even as I was writing this book, three years after COVID-19 was declared a pandemic, its effects on our industry were still rippling, and it appears that those ripples were wide and far reaching.

Because the business support sessions happened in an existential moment, my clients, colleagues, and friends were honest—really and truly honest—which allowed me to make great observations that I believe are felt or thought, whole or in part, by all yoga professionals. These observations are essential to our experience as yoga business owners and inextricably related to the future of the yoga business. I assessed that we were tired, we had sacrificed our priorities, we were making decisions based on "keeping up with the Joneses," we had forgotten our purpose, we were losing money rather than making it, and, most importantly, we vowed not to go back to the way things had been.

I believe that as an industry, we have arrived at a great moment, a moment where these assessments are worth considering and sitting with as we determine where we will go from here. I invite you now to pause, contemplate, observe, and assess your existing yoga business using a set of tools I've created to help you see, as clearly and thoroughly as possible, the state of your yoga business. These tools include a service model assessment, a visual identity assessment, a weekly workflow assessment, and a cash flow assessment. Getting to your next level starts here and now.

ASSESS YOUR SERVICE MODELS

Asking questions and gathering data about the service model you use in your current business will give you a realistic foundation on which to build your future business. Within the data you will look for patterns and trends and for what is missing. This will reveal clear opportunities for growth. The data will show what is really hap-

An honest, granular, and comprehensive assessment of your business is vital for getting to the next level.

pening in your yoga business, not what you *think* is happening. As entrepreneurs, we often tell ourselves stories about our businesses. The truth of these stories can be skewed if we focus on what's wrong and have trouble seeing what is going well or if we have in our head that things are humming along just fine when there are vital areas for improvement in the business that need to be addressed. An honest, comprehensive, and granular assessment will tell you the facts about your business, and usually things aren't as good or as bad as you think. It's much better to know the truth than to operate a small business based on a story that relies on unsubstantiated assumptions because most of us don't have a lot of backup resources to rely on when things go awry.

Take a look at figure 10.1. The horizontal rows of the worksheet are your service models and the vertical columns are the areas of assessment within each service model. Your assignment is to write down information in the appropriate box about where you are; this will form your assessment.

FIGURE 10.1 Service Model Assessment Worksheet

Service model	Analysis	Revenue (+)	Expenses (–)	Satisfaction	Questions to answer
One-to-one sessions					
Group sessions					
Conferences and festivals					
Workshops					
Immersions					
Retreats					
Trainings					
Products and merchandise					

From A. Taylor, *Your Yoga Business*. (Champaign, IL: Human Kinetics, 2024). Available online on HK*Propel*.

Let's look closer at each area of your current business assessment worksheet:

Analysis

This is where you will list general details about the business or lack of business you have in each service model. For example, if you have two private clients, you will write that in the one-to-one cell. Or if you teach four yoga classes each week, two online and two in person, you will write that in the group sessions cell. For the event-based service models, list what is scheduled, not events that you are thinking about leading. What are the first thoughts that come to mind when you think about each service model?

Revenue and Expenses

This is where you list the amount of money you are generating (+) or spending (−). For example, if you earn $150 per week, $600 per month, or $7,200 per year from those two private clients, you would write this information in the (+) column. If you spend $150 per month on gas to drive back and forth to those private clients, you would write that information in the (−) column. Ask yourself if you are making the kind of money that you want to make or feel that you could make in each service model. Does the money allow you to reinvest and grow your business? Does it allow you to contribute to the world in your highest capacity? We will do a detailed cash flow analysis of your overall business later in the chapter. Please log the approximate amounts of your annual revenue and expenses by service model. These figures will culminate in an annual income. We will take a more granular look at your revenue and expenses when we assess your cash flow. The purpose of this task is to give you a high-level look at your overall revenue and expenses by service model.

Satisfaction

Are you satisfied with where you are in this service model? Is this area of the business supporting your lifestyle, your family life, your health? Are you excited about this area of your business or the prospects to grow this area of your business? Be sure to ask yourself why you are or aren't excited about the possibilities within each service model.

Questions to Answer

What can you do to make this area of your business more profitable or more satisfying? Write that in the space as well. Are there ideal things about where you are in a particular service model (e.g., great pay for that one-to-one session!) or are there not-so-ideal things about where you are (e.g., a terrible schedule for the one-to-one session and the client cancels often)?

Remember, it's OK if you don't have input for every cell. Many yogis do not do it all. The point is to look clearly at what you have going on right now by taking the time to pause, contemplate, observe, and assess. You will quickly start to see how implementing simple shifts across all of your service models can create more opportunity and revenue for yourself.

Your Yoga Business Homework
Reflect on Your Current Business Service Models

When you've completed the assessment, take time to think about where your business is right now. Reflect on what you have accomplished, all the wins, all the losses, and all the learnings. It is powerful and important to process what you have accomplished, to celebrate what you have created, and to honor the lessons that you have learned the hard way before getting to work on the next steps, solutions, and opportunities that will get you to the next level.

Take some time to journal the reflections you have when you look at your current businesses service models. How do you feel about what you have accomplished? What have you learned along the way in terms of building out these elements of your business? What mistakes were made? What were your greatest successes?

____

____

____

____

____

____

ASSESS YOUR VISUAL IDENTITY

In the next step of your assessment process we will assess the visual identity of your existing business across all of your current communication channels. We will assess both how your visual identity is working (function) and how it looks (form). This process will give us the view from 30,000 feet that we chatted about in chapter 3 and will allow us to measure how your existing visual brand compares to the visual brand of your dreams. It's an important opportunity to create cohesion and make sure that all of your communication channels are working together effectively for your business. Through this process, you will be able to identify opportunities for improvement as well as to see which channels are working for you and which channels are not.

Open each of your communication channels on your computer: your website, Instagram, YouTube channel, and so on. Use the largest screen possible and simultaneously lay out all of your hard copy materials on your desk or a table in your physical work space: your postcards, business cards, ebooks, and manuals. The goal is to put as many components of your visual identity in front of you at the same time as you can as you begin the assessment. Also, don't forget to grab the visual cues mood board you created in chapter 3 and place it on the table alongside your other hard copy materials. This will allow you to compare the visual cues of your dream brand to your existing brand, which will help inspire you to complete your assessment even more robustly.

Let's look at the elements of your visual identity assessment worksheet (see figure 10.2). For the section of figure 10.2 that focuses on function, or how your visual identity is working for each communication channel, you'll see these columns:

Frequency of Use

Do you use the channel regularly? Many of us have a channel that is used infrequently or not at all. An unused channel is of no use, so if you can't commit to using it regularly, shut it down. Like my granny would say, "Don't be half a**ing it."

Consistency of Content

Is your information presented in a hodgepodge manner, or is it easy to see the pillars of your content? If someone new were to come to your channel and look back over the past two weeks of content, would they know what your business is all about? Creating more consistent messaging is an easy way to move your business to the next level. We'll come back to this when you build your business plan.

Visual Consistency

When you look at your channels side by side, do they look related, as if they are part of the same family? Or does it look like each channel could be a family of its own? Describe specifically what you could do to improve the visual consistency of each channel in relationship to the others. Whether you typically view them from 30,000 feet or not, their sum is your brand, and as we discussed in chapter 3, there should be cohesion for maximum brand recognition.

Accuracy of Information

Is all of your current data listed, such as your about info and contact details? This is important. You do not want to lose a potential client because your phone number or email cannot be easily found on all of your points of contact.

For the section of figure 10.2 that focuses on form, or how your visual identity for each communication channel looks, you'll see columns for purpose, pillars, personality, colors, font size and type, and key imagery. For a refresher, take a peek back at chapter 3 where we covered these elements of your visual identity in detail.

Now, we are ready to begin the visual identity assessment (see figure 10.2). Working through a column at a time, use the worksheet to identify and gather notes on what you are doing well and areas of improvement for each communication channel. To help you get started, here are a few examples of common assessments:

Frequency of use: You post frequently on Instagram, but you send out newsletters sporadically.

Accuracy of information: You don't list contact details on the about section of your YouTube channel, and your address is outdated on your website.

Font size and type: You are using a different font on most of your communication channels.

Key imagery: There is no photo of you on your website, and your postcards use photos that are 10 years old.

This is your chance to take note of all the ways you can improve your visual identity's function and form and bring your existing brand closer to the brand of your dreams. Take your time and be thorough. Often when completing a visual identity assessment, yoga professionals focus on the things they could be doing better and not the things they are doing well. I encourage you to do both as you complete this exercise!

FIGURE 10.2 Visual Identity Assessment Worksheet

	Function				Form					
Communication channel	Frequency of use	Consistency of content	Visual consistency	Accuracy of information	Purpose	Pillars	Personality	Colors	Font type and size	Key imagery
Website										
YouTube										
Vimeo										
Facebook										
Twitter										
Instagram										
Snapchat										
Pinterest										
Instagram										
Pinterest										
TikTok										

Communication channel	Function				Form					
	Frequency of use	Consistency of content	Visual consistency	Accuracy of information	Purpose	Pillars	Personality	Colors	Font type and size	Key imagery
LinkedIn										
Blogging and vlogging										
Email										
Newsletter										
Podcast										
Text										
SEO										
Paid advertising										
E-commerce										
Hard copy content (business cards, posters, fliers, postcards)										

From A. Taylor, *Your Yoga Business*. (Champaign, IL: Human Kinetics, 2024). Available online on HK*Propel*.

ASSESS YOUR WEEKLY WORKFLOW

Next you will assess your weekly workflow by taking a closer look at how *you* are showing up each day to run your yoga business. (You didn't think you were going to level up without making changes to your own behavior, did you?!) Too often I hear my clients say, "I don't have time to work *on* my business; I am so busy being *in* it." This is a difficult reality when you are growing your business. Leveling up requires that you dedicate time to work *on* your business, so it is crucial to find the time and space you need. In chapter 19, you will look more closely at what your dedicated work time needs to include.

The weekly workflow assessment is one of my favorite and most liberating exercises because it becomes a clear mirror that reflects how yoga professionals spend their time. Conducting the weekly workflow assessment allows you to see inefficiencies in your schedule and opportunities to be more productive and to streamline or eliminate activities in order to carve out more time for working on your business. The time you need is there, you just need to make shifts in order to gather it.

To assess your weekly workflow, write down everything you do for seven days (take a look at figure 10.3 for a sample weekly workflow). From waking to sleeping, record where, how, with whom, and on what you are spending your time. Include all of your personal, work, and family obligations as well as social and recreational activities. Be honest about your seven days. This only works when you tell the truth about how much news you read every day or how much time you really spend on Facebook! Don't be scared of the truth. Whether you complete the seven-day exercise on paper—yes, I still use paper—or take notes on your smartphone, you need to see the brutal truth about where, how, with whom, and on what you spend your time. Most smartphones have a screen time function that allows you to see in detail how much time you spend on your phone and on what activities, or you can use a productivity app to clearly track the time you spend on your computer.

FIGURE 10.3 Sample Weekly Workflow

	Monday	Tuesday	Wednesday	Thursday	Friday	Saturday	Sunday
8:00 am	Morning routine						
9:00 am	Instagram	Commute	Instagram	Instagram	Instagram	Instagram	Instagram
10:00 am	Group (90 min)	One-to-one (60 min)		Group (90 min)	Group (90 min)	Yoga	Cooking and meal prep
11:00 am		Commute					
12:00 pm	Lunch						
1:00 pm	Admin and email	One-to-one (60 min)					
2:00 pm			Coffee with Erica	Virtual group (60 min)	Coffee with Erica	Virtual group (60 min)	Virtual group (60 min)
3:00 pm		Commute					
4:00 pm		One-to-one (60 min)				One-to-one (60 min)	
5:00 pm							
6:00 pm		Gym		Gym		Errands and shopping	
7:00 pm	Dinner						
8:00 pm	Instagram and email	Instagram and email	Instagram	Admin and Netflix	Time with friends		
9:00 pm			Instagram				
10:00 pm			Instagram				
11:00 pm			Instagram				
12:00 am			Instagram				

From A. Taylor, *Your Yoga Business*. (Champaign, IL: Human Kinetics, 2024). Available online on HK*Propel*.

Your Yoga Business Homework

Reflect on Your Weekly Workflow

In this activity, you will download the blank weekly workflow template from HK*Propel* (instructions are provided at the front of this book) and track your weekly workflow for seven days.

After you have tracked everything you do for seven days, review your notes, and even consider showing them to a friend. Oftentimes we cannot see our reflection objectively, which is why showing a friend the outcome of your workflow assessment may provide additional insight and opportunities to make shifts. While you reflect, ask yourself these questions:

- Are there places where I am losing valuable time? I once had a client who was driving home in the middle of the day to let her dog out, costing her a minimum of two hours a day during peak office hours—if she didn't get caught watching TV. We got her a dog walker for $15 per day that gave her 10 more hours of office time per week, making her significantly more productive.
- Are there areas where my schedule hasn't changed in a long time that I can look at anew? Your class schedule and one-to-one schedule often create awkward gaps in your workweek that make it difficult to find concentrated time for working *on* the business. Perhaps you can shift a class or a client.
- Is there one thing in my day that makes the rest of that day or the week especially difficult to manage?
- Do I have too many meetings and not enough dedicated desk time?
- Has my own yoga practice disappeared from my week?

While you observe your existing week, get creative with what your ideal week could look like, and remember that everything is possible. One of the most powerful gifts that we were given by the pandemic was the opportunity to reallocate our time. Although we always had quite a bit of power to choose how we spent our days, the pandemic allowed many of our set structures to change (e.g., where we worked and went to school, how we got to work and got to school). It's now easier than ever to rethink how you are spending your time and to create an ideal schedule for yourself that suits both your personal and professional priorities.

Based on your observations, what one change can you make today that will give you more time for your business? Note that we will revamp your workweek even further later in chapter 19.

____

____

____

____

____

____

____

ASSESS YOUR CASH FLOW

Vinyasa flow, hatha flow, cash flow? In my perfect world, the words *cash flow* would be just as common as vinyasa and hatha. Unfortunately, this is not the case. Cash flow may be the least understood concept and least used tool in the yoga business—although it is an essential one. As a small-business owner, you need a business plan. This consists of financial documents that include sales projections and monthly cash flow and a marketing plan. We will work on developing them in the next chapter. I would not be doing my job if I didn't insist that from this point forward, you add cash flow management to your yoga business repertoire.

I have been surprised over the years by how many yoga business professionals would prefer to run their business by relying on instinct rather than planning and being methodical. Maybe their yoga practice helps them sleep at night. At any rate, you are here to learn how to move your business to the next level, and using a cash flow worksheet is an effective way to do so.

Figure 10.4 is a cash flow worksheet that, in its simplest terms, tracks the money that you make and the money that you spend each month in your business (you can download a blank formula-enabled worksheet from HK*Propel* using the instructions provided at the front of this book). This worksheet allows you to plan for your business needs in both the short and long term; as a matter of fact, you can look at your cash flow for an entire year at a time. The worksheet itself is self-explanatory, so let's spend time discussing what you are looking at when the worksheet is filled out. Each of the categories can be described this way:

- *Beginning cash*: How much money do have right now? Beginning cash refers to all money in your business's possession.
- *Projected income*: This is your expected cash inflow. How much cash do you expect to receive this month?
- *Projected expenses*: This is your expected cash outflow. What expenses do you anticipate this month? Keep in mind infrequent expenses that may only come up once or twice a year, such as membership dues or conference fees.
- *Forecasted cash*: Here is where you forecast the cash you expect to have on hand at the end of the month by adding your cash inflows to your beginning cash and subtracting your cash outflows.

You want your cash flow to be positive, meaning that your forecasted cash is a positive amount. When beginning to use this tool, it is common to see that there are months where your cash flow is negative—for example, you may be cash flow positive for the current month, but won't be six months from now. By using the worksheet, you can plan ahead for potential negative cash flows by asking the following:

- What can I do to adjust it and make it positive?
- Where can I trim my expenses, or where can I increase my revenue?

Having this level of awareness of your business and being able to anticipate cash flow fluctuations give you the power to mitigate damage to your business. There's nothing worse than being short on cash for the month and not having a plan in place to deal with it.

Using a cash flow worksheet also clarifies for you how much the business needs to be earning each month to cover the expenses and to pay you a salary. Yes, you need to be paid in order to be considered a business. There is a line item for salary

FIGURE 10.4 Cash Flow Worksheet

Beginning cash	Amount ($)	Projected income	Amount ($)	Projected expenses	Amount ($)	Forecasted cash	Amount ($)
Current cash balance		Available loan proceeds		Advertising		Current cash balance	
		One-to-ones		Financial service charges		Projected cash inflows (income)	
		Group sessions		Insurance		Projected cash outflows (expenses)	
		Conferences and festivals		Salary (your own)			
		Workshops		Payroll			
		Retreats		Payroll taxes			
		Immersions		Rent or lease			
		Trainings		Subscriptions or dues			
		Products		Supplies			
		Merchandise		Taxes and licenses			
		Savings		Utilities and telephone			
		Other		Travel			
				Other			
Total		Total		Total		Ending cash balance	

From A. Taylor, *Your Yoga Business*. (Champaign, IL: Human Kinetics, 2024). Available online on HK*Propel*.

under projected cash outflows and this salary is yours. What kind of cash inflow do you need to be able to pay yourself the salary that you are worth? It is from this position of clarity that you will set your financial goals. It's sort of an "if you build it, it will come" approach, and it works because using a cash flow tool also helps you to make more money. The more often you look at your numbers, the more you will see opportunities to create, market, and sell. I look at my cash flow almost every day—to keep fine-tuning, to keep motivated to sell, and to stay in touch with the reality of what is happening with my business.

Your Yoga Business Homework

Reflect on Your Cash Flow

In this activity, you will download the blank cash flow worksheet template from HK*Propel* (instructions are provided at the front of this book). Once you have the worksheet open, copy it so that you have three months of blank worksheets in front of you. Input your data for the next three months and then ask yourself the following series of questions:

Am I cash positive each month? ______________________________

____

Am I cash positive at the end of the three months? ________________

____

If I am not cash positive, are there ways I can impact sales of existing products and events to increase cash inflow in the short term? ____________________

____

____

Are there any shifts I can make to my expenses to help reduce costs? For example, am I overspending on advertising or continuing to pay for an unused subscription?

____

____

What is my current salary? How does this amount compare to what I am worth or what I would like to be earning? ______________________________

____

____

It is from this point of inquiry that we will work together on setting longer-term financial goals in the next chapter. But for now, as you can see from your answers, there are some immediate actions you can take to make your cash flow healthier in the short term.

What a chapter! We've assessed your current service models, your visual identity, your weekly workflow, and your monthly cash flow. This evaluation of where your business is at and what it is composed of in granular detail is literally the foundation upon which you will stand in order to reach the next level of your business. Congratulations, I know it was a lot of work. It gets easier to assess your business from here forward and I truly hope you feel empowered by the assessment process and can see all of the hard work you've put into your business and all of the opportunity that lies in front of you. You are now ready to begin building the business of your dreams!

11
SET GOALS

Society, family, and media combine to set standards of success or failure. Acceptance or rejection depends upon set rules of behavior and speech. The individual is constantly pulled away from his sense of uniqueness . . . even as we say aloud "uniqueness of the individual" we recognize how little we hear, let alone understand what these words mean at the deepest level.

T.K.V. Desikachar

In parts I and II, we established that great accomplishments start with great dreams, and we learned that becoming your dream is the result of three stages: your beginning, your destination, and the effort you put in to get there.

In chapter 10, we did a deep dive into assessing your starting point. You are now at the second stage, choosing your destination, or as some prefer to say, "asking the universe for what you want." I prefer to use the verb *choose* because to choose means that your dream is yours for the taking, whereas to *ask* means that you need permission granted in order to achieve your dreams. I also like the verb *choose* because you can hold it in your hand. You choose your destination by constructing crystal clear goals. These goals will form the business plan you will follow to get from where you are now to the next level of your business. Achieving these crystal clear goals is how you will build reality from your dreams.

DEFINE SUCCESS

First, I want to talk with you about success. In chapter 1, I asked you to consider, "Whose dreams are they?" to make absolutely sure that the dreams you are dreaming truly belong to you. In the same vein, I want to make sure that as you begin to set goals, your definition of success truly belongs to you. We often define success based on someone else's definition rather than considering what we really deem success to be. It's important to understand that success is relative, meaning that there is no standard that applies to everyone.

This means that my definition of success will be different from your definition of success, even though we might share the same dream. For example, our shared dream may be to become a full-time yoga teacher; however, the amount of money that I consider to be successful may not be the same as yours. It's crucial that I become my own dream and achieve my own definition of success, and it is crucial that you become yours.

So often we feel obligated to define our success based on other people's opinions rather than our own. So often in life we strive for someone else's definition of success rather than our own. I beg of you to choose your own destination and make these goals yours, especially when it comes to setting desired income.

Something else that I think is important when considering the success of your business is that your business is composed of many achievements, not a singular one, and that each of those achievements woven together holistically determine the success of your business. I call this reality the *fabric of success*. This concept developed out of a conversation I had with a yoga teacher, Dwayne Holliday, who asked me how I was doing. I was looking back with regret and *what iffing* my business decisions: What if I'd made a different decision? What if things had turned out differently? What if, what if, what if?

Success is relative: There is no standard that applies to everyone.

Sometimes, through the course of reflecting on lessons learned as a yoga business owner, we can dwell on the what ifs. I had sent myself down this rabbit hole by comparing the size of my business to the size of the businesses of some of my contemporaries. I started YAMA during a "founders moment" in New York City when an incredible number of wellness businesses were founded at the same time by folks who all knew each other—and YAMA was one of them. Many of these businesses had gone on to be publicly traded or acquired by larger companies, and there I was still a small business.

Dwayne's response to me was something to the effect of, "But look at what else you have: a happy relationship, a comfortable work-life balance, the opportunity to travel. You have great long-term client relationships and you still make all the decisions at YAMA." He was totally right. It immediately snapped me out of my pity party and helped me to realize that, first of all, I shouldn't have been comparing my business's success to that of another business—especially when looking from the outside in without knowing what was going on behind closed doors. And secondly, I couldn't just look at one area of my business in order to gauge my success. I had to look at all the achievements woven together to see how satisfied and successful I truly was.

It is so important when considering your dreams and defining success that you keep the business in full perspective. Accomplishing each goal has trade-offs: You may be spiritually fed but have an empty bank account. Conversely, you can have a full bank account and be totally miserable. There's a give-and-take to achieving your definition of success. So before you choose your destination, remember what you've identified so far about your priorities, and to the best of your ability, dream your own dreams and align your goals with your priorities and your definition of success.

MAXIMIZE YOUR BUSINESS

Getting your business to the next level doesn't necessarily mean that you have to reinvent yourself or massively innovate; getting to the next level can also happen by maximizing each area of your existing service models and making small but important modifications and adjustments. I want us to look at the opportunities you have to maximize your business before you set your goals.

I'll never forget the first time I met Leslie Kaminoff, the yoga educator and best-selling author. (Most people probably don't forget the first time that they met him either!) I was running late, *very late*, and still in the throes of being an ex-Angeleno learning how to commute and travel in the massive and unpredictable network of subways, buses, and taxis that is New York City. I was coming from Greenpoint, Brooklyn, which at that time won two prizes: cheapest rent and the least accessible apartments in the city. Starting YAMA not only required all of my courage and life-savings, but it also required quite a bit of personal sacrifice in those early years to keep my expenses and overhead as low as earthly possible while I waited to actually start making money.

Anyway, as you can see, I'm making up excuses for being late. None of which Leslie cared to listen to when I arrived gloriously at his office well-dressed and about 30 minutes past our appointment time. When I walked in, he was sitting on the couch considering me with curiosity, this upstart from out of town who was getting rave reviews from some well-respected yoga folks immediately upon landing in the city.

After I was done apologizing, he shared with me a bit about his business. I realized immediately that compared to what I was charging clients for the services of teachers with much less experience and name recognition than he had, he was substantially underpaid. When I let him know that I thought I could double his earnings without him having to change a thing about his business except his pricing, I was pretty much hired on the spot!

This is a great example of a small shift with a big impact, and this is what it means to maximize your business. There are many variables in your yoga business where a small and impactful shift is possible. These include the following (not an exhaustive list, but an essential one):

- *Price*—how much you charge for your services
- *Location*—where your services are offered
- *Frequency*—how often your services are offered
- *Platform*—how your services are delivered
- *Customers*—the kinds of students and businesses you serve
- *Expenses*—how much it costs you to run your business

Although I never lived down being late, because I'd successfully maximized Leslie's business, I ended up making an overall good impression!

Your Yoga Business Homework

Maximize Your Existing Business

Let's begin by using the service model assessment you completed in chapter 10 (see figure 10.1 on page 98) to review each of your service models through the lens of possible variables (e.g., price, location, frequency, platform, customers, expenses). As you work your way down the service model assessment, use the worksheet in figure 11.1 and write down possible adjustments (we will then use these findings in chapter 16 to further articulate strategies to reach your goals). Let's look at examples to get you started:

- *Price*—How would a shift in what you charge for your goods and services affect your incoming cash flow?
- *Location*—How would a change of location affect your service models? Consider new neighborhoods, cities, regions, and neighboring businesses.
- *Frequency*—What if you offered your services more frequently—for example, adding a second retreat each year or another group session each week? You may need to reduce the frequency of one of your service models in order to increase another—be mindful of how this affects your bottom line.
- *Platform*—Many yoga businesses are limited by platform issues. These can include a website without the ability to click to purchase, a virtual studio platform that does not allow the business to record and sell replays, or a platform that doesn't charge automatically for a monthly membership. All these issues limit revenue. Shifting to a new platform could increase the revenue without extra effort—other than the effort of changing platforms.
- *Customers*—Shifts in customers means accessing new audiences by diversifying your client base, which is an incredible opportunity to access new revenue. For example, perhaps your one-to-one clients are mostly C-level

executives. What would it look like to add other types of professionals such as lawyers or doctors?

- *Expenses*—Do you pay for expenses that you no longer use or need or could find another way to cover? For example, are you paying for software you don't use? Are you overpaying an assistant who was instrumental in helping you set up your business, but whose skills aren't needed anymore? Or, could you negotiate for your travel to be included when you host an international retreat? All these expenses add up and reduce overall profitability. Which of your expenses jump out as opportunities to reduce the costs associated with each service model?

FIGURE 11.1 Business Maximization Worksheet

Service model	Price	Location	Frequency	Platform	Customers	Expenses
One-to-one sessions						
Group sessions						
Conferences and festivals						
Workshops						
Immersions						
Retreats						
Trainings						
Products and merchandise						

From A. Taylor, *Your Yoga Business.* (Champaign, IL: Human Kinetics, 2024). Available online on HK*Propel*.

SET GOALS

I am a big fan of setting goals because they create clarity and yield results. Knowing the smaller components of your larger goals from the outset provides a realistic idea of what to expect and what is required to achieve those larger goals. This means that when you begin your journey, you know exactly what it will take to get there. This clarity breeds satisfaction because your own expectations have been met, and it leads to results as you accomplish each smaller goal.

Think big; act small.

It's sort of a *think big; act small* approach to business planning, which keeps your big dreams fully visible but places your day-to-day focus on the smaller goals that are readily achievable. This provides a great opportunity for accountability; you may not be able to see the final destination from where you are when you begin, but you can certainly record the milestones reached along the way. I don't think that when considering the distance your dreams will take your business that you can underestimate the importance of setting your goals well, setting your expectations well, and managing your pace well in between.

The goals we set will be in 24-month increments. Even before the pandemic, when we all lost our ability to plan ahead, I was not a fan of setting goals further ahead than that. Long-term vision I am OK with, but for me and my clients, I find that 24 months is an appropriate and manageable amount of time for achieving goals. It is far enough in the future to give you time to get things done but also close enough that you stay excited and inspired because your next level is close at hand.

Both of my grandmothers picked cotton. When I set goals, having a visual reminder on my desk—like this cotton I am holding—allows me to be grateful and focused on my priorities.

Real Talk

"The past 12 years of business have shown me patience—especially with new ideas. I don't rush into things at all. I consider them, examine the efficacy of them, plan them, and then take my time before diving in."
Finlay Wilson
Founder of Heart Space, a yoga not-for-profit, and creator of Kilted Yoga

Before we begin setting goals and discussing what stands in the way of accomplishing them—it's not always that you don't know what to do, it's often simply that you don't do it—let's take a look at the five qualities that great goals are made of. After all, we need great goals to achieve great dreams. These qualities are specific, measurable, attainable, realistic, and timely, also known as SMART goals.

Specific

What exactly is it that I want to accomplish? What exactly is it that I want my students to achieve? Why is this goal important? Who is involved? Where is it located? Which resources or limits are involved, and how are these resources going to be allocated? For example, if you need to raise money, you need to be specific about how much you need to raise and also how you will spend it. Get into the details!

Measurable

How will I know whether I have reached my goal? How will I know when I am successful? It's not enough to say you want to get to the next level; you need to quantify exactly what that next level is. Is it the desire to make more money in a particular service model? If so, how much more? Reach more students? How many? How will you know whether your students are successful? What are your goals for your students?

Achievable

Can I accomplish this goal? Am I giving myself enough time to do so? Do I have the skills required, the talent, the opportunity, or the financial means? Is this goal sustainable for me? As we discussed when we were dreaming our great dreams in chapter 1, you can absolutely dream past your current circumstance, but your goals need to be the realistic steps you will take to get there. So if your great dream is to become Beyoncé—there is dance and voice training, production of a demo tape, and forming your first band that will need to be accomplished, likely a decade's worth of smaller achievable goals that combine to create your great dream.

Relevant

A relevant goal can answer "yes" to these questions: Does this seem worthwhile? Is this the right time? Is this goal in alignment with other circumstances in your life? Am I the right person to reach this goal? Will this serve what my clients need at this very moment? I love thinking about relevance, particularly in the face of the unprecedented flux in our business environment. Is this the right time to be pursuing certain goals, or does the world ask us to reidentify our goals based on external circumstances? For example, many yoga teachers approached me during the early years of the pandemic looking to grow their conference and festival service model. I let them know that while that was a great goal, because of the pandemic, the conference and festival space (like most live entertainment-based industries) had been decimated and to turn their attention to the part of their business they could cultivate at that moment, such as creating content, until the market returned to normal.

Timely

To set a timely goal and the corresponding subgoals, start by determining when the main goal will be accomplished. To set your subgoals, work backward and ask yourself this: What will I have accomplished six months from now? What do I want to have achieved six weeks from now? What can I do today?

Now that you've reviewed what makes goals great, take a look at the obstacles to reaching your goals. Although the process is pretty simple—set goals and go after them—many of us don't accomplish much. We end up maintaining the status quo, or we lose enthusiasm. So why aren't we more effective at achieving our goals? It's not always that we don't know what to do; it's often simply that we don't do it. Here are some of the reasons why we do not achieve more goals:

Lack of stamina and unrealistic expectations.

This is otherwise known as running out of steam. A lot of yoga business owners hit a point of fatigue and frustration that keeps them from achieving their goals. Often, the reason they run out of steam is because they had no idea how much steam it would take to begin with. I recommend talking to someone who has accomplished the goal you're setting out to achieve to see what their process and timeline were like. There's nothing worse than having an unrealistic expectation. In business, I prefer to know clearly what I'm getting into before I get into it. Imagine starting a journey and knowing your final destination, but not having any idea how far away it is.

Focusing too far ahead.

Yes, your career is a marathon, and you want to keep the finish line top of mind, but on a day-to-day basis, staring at the distant finish line can be debilitating rather than motivating. Better to focus no further ahead than the next mile marker.

Failing to celebrate the smaller achievements along the way.

I love watching marathons and the epic finishes when the runners have finally accomplished this tremendous goal. Talk about a party! Yet one of the most endearing parts of watching a marathon is the fans celebrating and cheering the runners along, every step of the way, one mile at a time. Keeping a spirit of celebration in your business at each milestone helps keep you going when the race is long.

Getting off course.

It is understood that dreams and goals change. However, many yoga business owners set SMART goals and then change their minds based on not much more than a whim. Maybe they see someone using a different strategy or platform and think that it is the better way to proceed rather than sticking to their own plans. I often see folks trying to keep up with other people's dreams and successes and changing their own dreams and goals to match. Give your dreams and goals time to work or to fail before you set a new course of action.

Suffering from perfection infection.

Done is better than perfect.

Many of us suffer from varying degrees of perfectionism, which is paralyzing when working toward larger goals. I will be honest, it took me a while to accept that done is better than perfect and to understand that it isn't usually the best who reaches the finish line first, it's the one who starts early. I am not saying to sacrifice integrity or quality in your business, but if you keep waiting until you are ready or until conditions are perfect to take steps to move your business forward, you risk falling behind people who are less qualified than you and risk missing out on opportunities to learn along the way because you are still at the starting gate.

Goals and deadlines mean very little if you suffer from a perfection infection that keeps you from finishing your smaller goals. You have to be able to say, "It's done," so that you can take the next step toward the goal. For example, I witnessed a teacher spend years on a new website to strengthen their visual brand presence before they allowed themselves to pitch brands for partnerships. I always wonder what opportunities they missed out on and what they would have gained if they'd said the website was "done" earlier and had allowed themselves to move on to the next step of becoming their dream. Take a look at figure 11.2 for a sample set of 24-month goals derived from dream goals.

FIGURE 11.2 Sample Build Your Dreams Worksheet: 24-Month Goals

Service model	24-month goal	Dream goal	By when?
One-to-one sessions	Sell 100 private sessions at $150 per session	Earn $25,000 per year	6 years
Group sessions	Increase revenue	Earn $50,000 per year	6 years
Conferences and festivals	Pitch myself to 10 conferences or festivals	Teach at two conferences or festivals per year and earn $5,000	6 years
Workshops	Sell two weekend workshops per year	travel four times a year to lead workshops and earn $10,000	24 months
Immersions			
Retreats	Connect with three key contacts about their experience running retreats and ask for a recommendation of location; exchange for social media posts of their upcoming retreats	Host one retreat and have one week vacation each year and earn $12,500	24 months
Trainings	Research 300-hour training programs	Become a teacher trainer with 20 graduates per year and earn $35,000	10 years
Products and merchandise	Add a writing block once a month to my schedule	Become a published author	6 years
	Add landing page with free offer to my website	Secure a paid ambassador relationship with one of my favorite brands; email list of 10,000	6 years

Your Yoga Business Homework

Articulate Your Dreams

Now it's your turn to articulate your dreams and to break them into realistic and manageable 24-month goals that will put you well on your way to reaching your dream destination! Many dream goals will take longer than 24 months to accomplish, and that is OK. Your aim here is to think big and act small as you journey towards your dreams.

Using the dreams that you organized in chapter 1, create clear 24-month goals for each of your service models. Remember, this is your definition of success, not anyone else's. What goal can you arrive at 24 months from now that will help you to achieve a significant milestone on the way to your dream destination?

Using figure 11.3, create 24-month goals for each of your service models working backwards from your dream goals.

FIGURE 11.3 Build Your Dreams Worksheet: 24-Month Goals

Service model	24-month goal	Dream goal	By when?
One-to-one sessions			
Group sessions			
Conferences and festivals			
Workshops			
Immersions			
Retreats			
Trainings			
Products and merchandise			

From A. Taylor, *Your Yoga Business*. (Champaign, IL: Human Kinetics, 2024). Available online on *HKPropel*.

Setting goals is an underestimated and often overplayed task. People talk about setting goals so much that it loses its luster and some of its power. Yet the act of dreaming and choosing that which you would become boils down to goal setting, and that is essentially the ultimate task. What can be more important than defining what success means to you? What can be more important than the journey to become your dreams, even if you get lost along the way?

The arc of a career and the arc of a lifetime if we listen closely to the contents of our dreams is the North Star which leads us to happiness. It is for this reason that the process of setting goals is so important and not to be taken lightly. I wish you well in your journey toward your dreams.

12
CONNECT YOUR CONTENT

In part I, you identified your purpose, wrote a remarkable bio, created a tagline, branded your weird, and extracted your pillars. All of this work and the materials that you created are the foundation of your yoga business from which we will further develop your overall business. This foundational material is also what is considered *content*: the messages, information, and experiences you share with your audience and students through your service models and communication channels; your content literally is your yoga business.

Two types of content are at work in your yoga business: paid and free. Paid content refers to the messages, information, and experiences you sell to your audience and students, and free content refers to the messages, information, and experiences that you give away at no cost in order to build an audience and attract students.

There is an inextricable tie between what you give and what you sell.

There is an inextricable tie between what you give and what you sell. I call this inextricable tie a *content connection*, and the more robust the content connection, the more successful the business. A well-thought-out and organized content connection allows you to give and sell across all of your service models, which keeps your students interested and buying within your business. It also answers a few questions I am asked all the time, such as "What should I be saying in my marketing?" and "What kinds of goods and services should I develop within my business?" The content connection is also a great opportunity to brand your goods and services. In the same way Sadie Nardini and I branded the Rock Your Yoga concept across all of her service models—turning ordinary workshops and retreats into something uniquely hers—so too can you create potent brand recognition in the market for your yoga business. We'll start by assessing and observing the paid and free content of my yoga business, and then we will assess the paid and free content of yours.

UNDERSTANDING PAID CONTENT

Take a look at the Content Connection Worksheet that I have begun in figure 12.1. This reflects my existing business and the goods and services that I currently offer, organized by the pillar they relate to (my pillars are empowerment, opportunity, and clarity of purpose and direction). The content you are looking at in this worksheet is my paid content—the messages, information, and experiences that people pay me to provide as they relate to my pillars. I love thinking about my business through the framework of the content connection because it allows me to see the great amount of opportunity to build paid content that exists under each pillar of my business. As we discussed earlier in our service model conversation, you do not need to develop your business in every single service model under your pillars just because you can. But each of the blank spaces is an area of opportunity to develop goods and services within your business.

FIGURE 12.1 Sample Content Connection Worksheet: Paid Content

Paid content	Pillar 1: Empowerment	Pillar 2: Opportunity	Pillar 3: Clarity of purpose and direction
One-to-one sessions	reBUILD consulting packages	Pitching consulting packages	Road Map consulting packages
Group sessions	reBUILD online studio classes	reBUILD online studio classes	reBUILD online studio classes
Conferences and festivals	reBUILD workshop	reBUILD workshop	reBUILD workshop
Workshops	reBUILD workshop	reBUILD workshop	reBUILD workshop
Immersions			
Retreats			
Trainings			
Products and merchandise	The Catalyst online business school for yogis reBUILD series (online) Your Yoga Business book and online access	The Catalyst online business school for yogis reBUILD series (online) Your Yoga Business book and online access	The Catalyst online business school for yogis reBUILD series (online) Your Yoga Business book and online access

So, let's have a look at what we can observe from my paid-content assessment. The first thing that jumps out at me are the blank spaces. My assessment clearly shows that there are opportunities for me to develop my business in the immersion, retreat, and training service models. There is also opportunity in the merchandise service model. I used to have a line of yoga clothes in our e-commerce shop that I could resurrect. Everyone loved those yoga hoodies! Another observation of my paid assessment is the solid name branding of the goods and services I offer. I don't just offer consulting packages; they have a signature brand name that only my yoga business uses, which makes my goods and services unique and stand out in the market. You can peek back to chapter 8 on menu of services for more on branding.

Your Yoga Business Homework

Assess Your Paid Content

Now it's your turn to assess the paid content that exists in your business. We will look for your blank space areas of opportunity and also assess opportunities for better branding across your goods and services. To begin, write your pillars across the top of figure 12.2 and then work your way down by adding your existing paid goods and services by service model under the appropriate pillar.

FIGURE 12.2 Content Connection Worksheet: Paid Content

Paid content		Pillar 1:	Pillar 2:	Pillar 3:
	One-to-one sessions			
	Group sessions			
	Conferences and festivals			
	Workshops			
	Immersions			
	Retreats			
	Trainings			
	Products and merchandise			

What do you observe on your paid-content connection worksheet, and what ideas do you have for acting on areas of opportunity? What other ways to diversify your business can you observe from the blank space on your content connection? How well are your paid goods and services branded? Is there room to improve the names of your goods and services? Make notes here:

UNDERSTANDING FREE CONTENT

To run your business properly, you also need to have content that you give away for free (we will talk much more in depth about this in part IV) that intentionally matches the content that you sell. Free content can be created in all formats and distributed via all communication channels, including events. In essence, you garner interest in your yoga business by giving away intriguing, provoking, educating, enlightening, and inspiring content *at no cost to the consumer*. I consider free content to be flirting with the market!

Now, let's take a look at the Content Connection Worksheet that I have begun in Figure 12.3. For each of my pillars, I have matched the content I give away for free within my yoga business. Here's a more detailed explanation of my existing free content:

- *Pillar 1: Empowerment.* I have a podcast, "Become Your Dream," that highlights the real stories of yoga professionals who have achieved their great dreams, and I also intentionally share images of strong female business owners and trailblazers to portray a sense of empowerment.
- *Pillar 2: Opportunity.* I share images of myself and clients doing things such as celebrating a book launch or a new studio opening to convey that the company creates opportunity.
- *Pillar 3: Clarity of purpose and direction.* Once a year, I host an online goal-setting event to support yoga teachers in creating clarity in their businesses.

FIGURE 12.3 Sample Content Connection Worksheet: Free Content

	Pillar 1: Empowerment	Pillar 2: Opportunity	Pillar 3: Clarity of purpose and direction
Free	"Become Your Dream" podcast	Share images of me and clients doing epic things!	Annual goal-setting event (online)
Free	Share images of strong female business owners and trailblazers	Annual networking event (in person)	Share goal setting success stories (1 per week)
Free			
Free			

Now, let's look at what we can observe in my free-content assessment and what could be created to make the most of the opportunity. The first thing that jumps out at me are the blank spaces. My assessment clearly shows I could add free content under the opportunity pillar. For example, as the pandemic is easing, but so few yoga events are happening and many studios are still closed, I think it's time to host an in-person networking event to build community and create opportunity. So I added annual networking event (in-person) under that pillar.

The clarity of purpose and direction pillar is important because it connects directly to my Road Map consulting packages, which are the best-selling products within my business. Therefore, the free content that connects to my best-selling products should be strong. So, for example, I added goal-setting success stories as a way to show the importance and effectiveness of the clarity of purpose and direction pillar as well as my own proficiency in supporting clients in being successful.

With regards to branding, I can see that both the annual online goal-setting event and the annual in-person networking event don't have brand names. Maybe I can make them all part of a "Become Your Dream" series. Whatever I decide, these free events need to be branded.

Your Yoga Business Homework

Assess Your Free Content

Now it's your turn to assess the free content that exists in your business. We will look for your blank space areas of opportunity and also assess opportunities for better branding across your goods and services. To begin, write your pillars across the top of figure 12.4 and then work your way down by adding your existing free goods and services by service model under the appropriate pillar.

FIGURE 12.4 Content Connection Worksheet: Free Content

	Pillar 1: ______	Pillar 2: ______	Pillar 3: ______
Free			
Free			
Free			
Free			

What do you observe on your free-content connection worksheet, and what ideas do you have for acting on the areas of opportunity? What other ways could you diversify your free-content marketing? How well are your paid goods and services branded? Is there room to improve the names of your goods and services? Make notes here:

____

____

____

____

____

____

____

There is an inextricable link between what you give away and what you sell. Now that you have completed the work in this chapter, you can see how both halves of your business relate to each other and how one without the other is incomplete. Your paid and free content depend on each other. Paid content without free content won't sell, and free content without paid content isn't a for-profit business. All of your paid and free goods and services can be branded to give your business a unique presentation in the market. We will return to your content connection observations in chapter 18, Identify Strategies. Next we will explore marketing.

PART IV
REFINE YOUR MESSAGE

13
GRASSROOTS MARKETING

Having a great message and a great product is the first step to creating a great yoga business, so congratulations on getting this far! Now it's time to get your message and your product out into the world. Getting your product out into the world requires consistency and courage, although even the most confident yoga business owners will tell you that the true key to their marketing success is strategy, planning, and execution.

In the next few chapters, I'll dive deep into the types of marketing channels available and review the best practices you'll need in order to master them to promote your yoga business. I will cover the essential information you need for impactful in-person and online marketing, discuss hot-button marketing conversations buzzing in the yoga space, and I'll share two key tools for properly planning and staying accountable to your marketing: a well-organized folder of assets and a marketing schedule. I encourage you to think about spending as much time, energy, and money honing your marketing as you do honing your craft as a teacher.

So, let's start at the beginning with grassroots marketing. Grassroots marketing (also known as guerrilla marketing or word-of-mouth marketing) starts from the ground up and is the core of marketing in the yoga business. Instead of launching a message with the aim of appealing to many people, your efforts are targeted to a small group with the hope that the small group spreads your message to a larger audience. This is why every student matters, and why every network, no matter the size, has massive potential.

ONE STUDENT AT A TIME

To explain the importance of this type of marketing, I'll share a quick story. There's a photo of me with my hair in pigtails, and I'm wearing a metallic electric-orange sports bra and a pair of lululemon's famous groove pants, and I'm doing triangle pose outside with my friend Gabe. If that in itself doesn't sound crazy, it's where I was doing that triangle pose that really makes the story!

Gabe and I and a handful of other educators from the Beverly Hills lululemon store where I worked at the time decided to do what we called "guerilla yoga" to attract new students to the store, and we figured where better to do it than in the middle of Avenue of the Stars, one of the flashiest streets in Los Angeles. Avenue of the Stars is home to Creative Artists Agency, the world's largest talent agency, which we used to jokingly call "the house that Oprah built." And there I was in all my black-stretchy-pants glory doing yoga on the median. Little did I know that three short years later I'd be walking into CAA to take a meeting with the head of new business development after starting YAMA.

When I think back on it now, I laugh; I was so in love with my job and on a mission to spread yoga that I didn't care what anybody thought about me. I was fearlessly passionate and willing to do just about anything it took to get people talking and to get them into the store. Not only did we get them talking, but we also literally stopped traffic. One after the other, people smiled or shook their heads in disbelief, some took photos, and all of them asked us, "What on earth are you doing?" We, of course, told them about the benefits of yoga and invited them to join us for a class at the new store with the funny name that no one could pronounce. And they would come to see us. Then they would tell a friend, who would tell a friend, who would come to see us, too.

Real Talk

"That's right. You learn from those five students, and they may have a fantastic experience and go tell five other people what a wonderful yoga session they had."
Anodea Judith
Author, public speaker, and therapist

We built the business like this, one conversation at a time (no website or social media!) until we had pretty much taken over the entire fitness scene in Los Angeles. Our one small group of loyal believers spread the message to a very large audience. Using word-of-mouth marketing is a powerful and important way to help grow your yoga business—and I do not believe that its importance has lessened with the emergence of social media but rather that the two, when used well, are quite complementary.

Getting people talking and beginning to harness the power of grassroots marketing starts with engaging in simple conversation. You have to be the first believer. The more you engage in conversation, the more likely you are to find others who believe what you believe. When they become evangelized believers in your yoga business, then they too begin doing the work of getting your message out into the world. Having these believers also talking about your yoga business amplifies your time and energy and allows you to benefit from the networks of your followers, too.

It may seem a bit old school to work on grassroots marketing when you have access to all the new ways to connect and market yourself online. But there is a real power in getting vocal and getting local. A smart yoga business owner will not leave any opportunity to market themselves untapped, and a consistent grassroots marketing effort goes a very long way.

Grassroots marketing is all about taking it to the streets!

BEST PRACTICES FOR GRASSROOTS MARKETING

In addition to doing yoga in the middle of the street, I have a host of other best practices for creating successful grassroots marketing. Let's take a look at some of them:

Share your good work with everyone around you.

Many of us think that because we feel that we are "putting ourselves out there" that everyone around us knows what we do. I assure you that this is not the case. It is your responsibility to share the good work that you are doing with everyone around you and to invite them to support your cause. Some of your own neighbors have no idea what you do; imagine the impact on your business if they were in the know and their immediate connections were also in the know. This ripple effect of converging networks is powerful. To be successful at grassroots marketing, you need to believe that everyone is a potential client or collaborator or that they know someone who could be.

Be confident.

Many yogis—although comfortable teaching in front of the room—find it difficult to talk about their services and what they offer with the people immediately around them. The majority of the people you need to reach in order to attain your goals are in the community right around you. Not being confident enough to engage them in a simple conversation can hold you back from business opportunities that are close at hand. Each business card exchanged or handshake given gets you one step closer to becoming your dreams. A great way to build the confidence to engage in conversation is to practice chatting people up. For some of us it comes more naturally to strike up spontaneous conversations, and for others it's a bit of a stretch. If you find it difficult to initiate conversation, you can practice with a friend by pretending you've just met and asking each other basic questions such as "What do you do for work? What do you do for fun?" These practice conversations will help you see how even the most basic interaction is an opportunity to promote your yoga business. Another great way to build confidence is by setting a goal to give out one business card a day until you find your groove and begin to chat with people and give out cards automatically.

The majority of the people you need to reach in order to attain your goals are in the community right around you.

Remember, it's a numbers game. If you give out 10 business cards, most likely 1 or 2 of those connections will convert and come to class, buy something from you, follow you online, sign up for your newsletter, and so on. Successful grassroots marketing depends on keeping your pipeline full of new leads. Keep a positive mindset while you engage by remembering that a small group of loyal followers can truly drive the business and by focusing not on the eight people who don't convert but on the two who do.

Be prepared.

Once you have gotten into your groove and are connecting on a personal level with everyone you come across, you have to be sure to have a way to keep in touch with those that you meet. So often we overhear business owners having a great conversation and then ending with "I left my business cards at home" or "I don't have a pen" or some other simple miss that keeps them from connecting with a potential client. Try to keep a stack of hard copy marketing material in your purse, backpack, or car, or invite someone to follow you on social media as a way to keep in touch. You never know when or where you will have the chance to win a new client, so it is best to be prepared to engage at all times. Refer to the event marketing checklist in chapter 15 for a complete list of hard copy marketing materials that your business should always have available.

You never know when or where you will have the chance to win a new client, so it is best to be prepared to engage at all times.

Make connecting with people a habit.

Give out five business cards and invite five people to follow you on social media in a week. By accomplishing the goal of acquiring 10 new grassroots connections in one week you will start to train yourself to be comfortable connecting on a regular basis. By the end of the week you'll be inspired and confident and have new client leads and new opportunities for your yoga business, and you will probably have had a bit of fun. We will make a list of places you can find your new grassroots connections in the homework exercise below.

I love to give out business cards in the reception area of yoga studios, local yoga apparel stores, in line at my favorite coffee shops, and farmer's markets. I also end up chatting with folks on the subway or at the local wine bar. Because yoga is for everyone, every person you come across is a potential client. Once you start to think of making connections that way, your business cards will almost always need replenishing. This also applies to social media. If you are in someone's orbit and find yourself commenting on their feeds or sharing their content, or you see people commenting on or sharing yours, seal the deal and ask them to follow you. When someone makes the effort to ask me to follow them, I almost always do. You won't get to a million followers this way, and that is not the point. The point is to get comfortable making connections.

Your Yoga Business Homework

Brainstorm Grassroots Marketing Opportunities

Think about all the places that yogis and health-minded folks hang out in town. Where do they eat, where do they shop for food and clothes, and where do they socialize? Make a list of five ideal places to give out business cards.

1. ____________________
2. ____________________
3. ____________________
4. ____________________
5. ____________________

A single coffee shop conversation or direct message on Instagram can start your official grassroots marketing campaign, so keep in mind the massive potential of a small group of believers to spread your message to a very large audience. A one-student-at-a-time approach is an empowering and important way to live your marketing each day. Be prepared and be confident because the majority of the people you need to reach in order to attain your goals are in the community right around you! Now that we've taken a thorough look at how to market your yoga business on a grassroots level, it's time to dive into digital and social media marketing in the next chapter.

14 DIGITAL AND SOCIAL MEDIA MARKETING

I started practicing yoga and had studied and worked in advertising and marketing for well over a decade before the public adopted the Internet. (Yes, I'm dating myself!) Even before the Internet, I was well versed in the use of advertising, marketing, and media to sway opinions and buying dollars. As someone who marketed yoga both before widespread use of the Internet and afterward, I can say that for a handful of years after marketing through the Internet became common, I thought that digital marketing was optional. I mean, the world did exist before the Internet after all, so who could blame me for holding on to such a wild notion? I understood that digital marketing was something you could do, but not something that you had to do in order to run a successful yoga business. Before the year 2000, almost all of the household name yoga teachers, studios, and brands had zero online presence.

Digital marketing is *marketing, and if you're not participating in digital marketing, you aren't really marketing at all.*

Fast-forward to now, and I would say that digital marketing *is* marketing, and if you're not participating in digital marketing, you aren't really marketing at all. Digital marketing is vast and comprises many communication channels, and most organizations could justify having a full-time person working solely on each communication channel.

But don't be intimidated, because you don't need to be a media professional to use them effectively, and you don't need to use them all. The learning curve for many of these channels is constantly changing, and even the savviest professionals are constantly learning and having to play catch-up. It reminds me of how a master yoga teacher says that "the more they teach, the less they know." Such is the nature of technology, and such is the nature of yoga. The point is to get on the digital marketing bus, do what you can to keep learning via trial and error, and commit to using some of these tools well.

We will begin with a digital marketing channel review. We'll use a checklist to see where you stack up. Each marketing channel on the checklist is technically different from the other, but the overall concept is the same: A group of people are hanging out in a place, and you are trying to connect with them by creating content for them to consume. Some of the groups are public, like social media platforms. Some of the groups are private, such as an email list that you have built and cultivated. I won't get super technical about each of the channels and how they work because there are other books and information written by subject matter experts. Most of the channels also include robust help desks with technical support staff who will quickly and efficiently answer most questions that you may have about the functionality of the platform and best practices for how to perform well on the platform.

What I will focus on is how to use these communication channels well for your yoga business. This chapter will include a digital marketing channel overview, followed by best practices for digital marketing. I will also discuss the benefits and dangers of social media and provide a homework exercise to help you keep your digital marketing assets organized.

Real Talk

"I'm trying to fall in love with marketing, because that's where it's at these days. If you don't market, everything falls flat. Marketing wasn't what I was born to do. I was born to teach. But marketing goes with it."
Anodea Judith
Author, public speaker, and therapist

TYPES OF DIGITAL MARKETING

Digital marketing, also called online marketing, uses the Internet and other forms of digital communication. Here are the most common types:

- *Blogging and vlogging*: This involves writing articles or recording videos on specific topics that are housed either on your site or on a partner's website. Linking to your site from your partner's site via a backlink improves your search engine optimization score.
- *E-commerce*: Selling goods and services directly from your own website requires a site that is built to display goods and services and collect payments.
- *Email marketing*: By creating an opt-in email list you can communicate via newsletters. Email marketing can be automated to deliver a series of communications to specific customers for a certain purpose to help you achieve a specific goal. These automated campaigns are called drip campaigns and can be useful when you have certain customer types. For instance, brand-new customers or people interested in a teacher training or retreat would benefit from a tailored series of communications.
- *Podcasting*: These audio recordings are similar to miniature radio shows. Podcasts allow you to deliver content audibly rather than visually via text or video. They provide a great opportunity to collaborate with peers in your network by asking them to speak on your podcast.
- *Social media marketing*: You can use your social media channels to give away content and to sell products, and you can link from them to your store on your website. Some popular social media channels include Instagram, Facebook, TikTok, Snapchat, Pinterest, LinkedIn, YouTube, and Vimeo.
- *Text message marketing*: You can communicate business news, sales, promotions, and other relevant information to your customers via SMS (short message service) text messages to their mobile devices.
- *SEO (search engine optimization)*: SEO refers to how quickly your business's website or social media channels can be found in the results of a search engine (e.g.,Yahoo or Google) when someone is looking for a similarly worded product or company—for instance, "yoga teacher in your hometown" does your business come up in the search? Do you come up on the first page, or the tenth? This will give you an indication of how well SEO is performing in your business.
- *Paid advertising*: Creating ads that are connected to search terms will help people find your business's website or social media channels. It is a method to increase your SEO. You pay per click for people who see your ad and then click on the ad to land at your website or social media channel.

The world of digital marketing is wide and deep. Deciding how many digital marketing channels are right for you depends on how much time you or your team can commit to consistently creating and posting content. Remember that marketing, while crucial, is just one of the essential elements of a successful business. Investing your time and money too heavily in it at the expense of other business-related activities can be harmful in the long run.

Your Yoga Business Homework

Take Stock of Your Digital Marketing

Using figure 14.01, the digital marketing inventory worksheet, check the box in the first column to denote if the digital marketing element is currently in use in your business and then list the frequency in the second column (high, medium, low, or rarely). This will help you to see how much you are or aren't leveraging digital marketing in your business and if you are consistent with those channels. Both observations are key areas of growth for your business.

FIGURE 14.1 Digital Marketing Inventory Worksheet

Digital marketing channel	Do I use it now?	Frequency of use
Blogging and vlogging		
Email		
Newsletter		
Podcast		
Text		
SEO		
Paid advertising		
E-commerce		
YouTube		
Vimeo		
Facebook		
Twitter		
Instagram		
Snapchat		
Pinterest		
TikTok		
LinkedIn		
Other		

From A. Taylor, *Your Yoga Business*. (Champaign, IL: Human Kinetics, 2024). Available online on HK*Propel*.

THE BENEFITS AND DANGERS OF DIGITAL MARKETING AND SOCIAL MEDIA

All of the communication channels we've discussed are relatively new, and the reality is that we don't know what the long-term effects of living and communicating in a digital world will be. What I do know is based on my personal experience and what I've learned from my clients, community, and peers through direct conversation, observation, and business interactions both formal and informal.

What I know is that digital marketing and social media are not all fun and games, and while these are now necessary tools to use to run your business, there are real benefits and also real dangers associated with doing so. Many of us in the yoga industry have an unhealthy relationship with digital marketing and social media, and these unhealthy relationships have consequences that affect our industry. We should be aware of both the benefits and dangers, for the sake of our students, our communities, and ourselves.

As I was writing this book, I explored my observations a bit further by anonymously questioning a group of yoga teachers on what they saw as the benefits and dangers of social media. The results of the inquiry were eye opening to me and the participants. By reflecting on the relationships we have with digital marketing and social media, we were able to find awareness, healing, and places where we could make shifts to create a healthier digital reality.

Based on my anonymous survey, here are some of the benefits of social media use:

- An opportunity to connect and deliver content and information to people near and far through an inexpensive (although time consuming) and democratized method of communication
- An opportunity to connect for business opportunities
- An additional revenue stream
- A modern calling card
- An opportunity to express oneself artistically, a place to be inspired
- An opportunity to connect, engage, share challenges, share successes, and share life

I agree that all of these are benefits and that digital marketing and social media will remain part of the yoga landscape, so we may as well make use of it while trying our hardest not to lose ourselves in the meantime. Speaking of losing ourselves, the responses I received from my survey on the dangers were much more in depth and telling than the responses about the benefits. I have condensed and organized the responses into the following paragraphs. I am curious whether you agree with these sentiments or have had any of these thoughts before. We all think everyone knows better than to think or react like the following examples, but I assure you, we do not and these sentiments are real answers from real yoga teachers like you.

Real Talk

"How many people are telling the ****ing truth about their life? What if I really told the truth!?"
Bryan Kest
Yoga practitioner, teacher, and creator of Power Yoga

Again, based on my anonymous survey, here are some dangers of social media use:

- *Comparison.* It's so easy to look at someone's channel and be filled with emotions such as envy and bitterness about the number of followers they have and their fabulous life. This constant comparison causes many yoga teachers to feel depressed after spending time on social media. Remember that what you see is not what you get, but rather that what you see is a carefully curated, filtered, and scripted version of reality. In reality, no one's life is better than yours. Do you compare yourself to other yoga teachers? Do you think they have a better life, business, or relationship than you do? Does social media make you feel depressed?
- *Valuation.* Yoga teachers often feel "less than" if they have a smaller following than another yoga teacher, and "better than" if they have a larger following than another yoga teacher. Students also assume and associate quality with audience size, which creates a confusing dynamic in the market. Just because a teacher has a larger following than another is no indication of their abilities. We assume everyone knows this and knows better than to value a yoga teacher in this way, but they do not. Another type of valuation that is dangerous is assuming that teachers with more followers are more financially successful. I know many teachers who have 100,000 followers and do not make $100,000 a year, and many teachers with many fewer than 100,000 followers who do make $100,000 a year. Ask yourself this: Do you feel that your value as a teacher is related to the size of your social media following?
- *Validation.* Of course, everyone wants to be liked. The quest for "likes" drives us to seek external validation rather than internal validation, which is the polar opposite of our yoga practice. Ask yourself this: What is your relationship with your sense of popularity online?
- *Copycat.* When spending time online, we are bombarded with the communication of our peers, colleagues, competitors, and random strangers, which is inspiring, distracting, and exhausting all at the same time. This bombardment of other people's content often leads us to think that we are not doing enough or should be doing this or that with our own communication. This causes us to jump from one thing to the next rather than following through on our own plans. It is difficult to execute and stay in your own lane when you are constantly trying to copycat another yoga teacher. Ask yourself who you would be online and how you would market your business if you could not see anyone else's communication.
- *Isolation.* Some yoga teachers spend more time online than in real life and withdraw from the yoga community and become isolated. Consider how much time you are spending online compared with how much time you are interacting in real life with your community. Are you spending more time with people online than in real life? Many of us, myself included, can benefit from more real-life connections.

I have found it useful to discuss the benefits and dangers of digital marketing and social media, both for myself and for my clients. Taking the time and creating the space for the conversation makes it important and requires that we pay attention to it, which is often the best way to prevent or mitigate danger.

BEST PRACTICES FOR DIGITAL MARKETING

It's been a joy and a huge learning experience to watch and support numerous yoga professionals build their online presence and master their digital marketing while also building up that of my own company. I've compiled the lessons learned into a set of best practices that will help you to understand the reality of what it takes to create a successful digital marketing campaign and tips that will help you see results more quickly. I am excited to share these best practices with you!

Be patient with your growth.

Everyone started at zero clients and followers. You have to trust that your audience will grow, and give it time to develop. Although growth in followers is an essential component of your business's success, it is not the only thing that makes your business a success. I have watched committed yogis authentically build their audiences from zero to tens or hundreds or thousands of followers. It takes courage to keep going when the growth is modest. Avoid the temptation to buy followers or email addresses. These shortcuts are more common than you would think, and I have never encouraged it as a growth strategy.

Be realistic.

Most of us won't have or won't need to have 100,000 followers to reach our goals. A small, dedicated, and engaged audience of students and followers can drive a successful business. Focus on who is in front of you rather than who is not.

Be you.

A lot of yogis get carried away emulating the posting style of someone who has a large audience, assuming that they must have figured out the magic formula for growing a huge following. It is one thing to be inspired by a teacher or a studio with

Luis Alvarez/ DigitalVision/Getty Images

This woman might be smiling, but digital marketing and social media are not all fun and games. It's important to be aware of the benefits and dangers as you run your yoga business.

a large following; it's another to become someone you're not just for the sake of trying to grow your following online. There is also a big difference between copying a channel's structure (such as frequency of posts, style or framing of photos, or use of different formats) and copying the messaging of the person you are emulating. No matter how big your audience, you will eventually become miserable if the messaging is not your own.

Accept the haters.

If you are really being you, then the truth is that not everyone will like you. The more you extend yourself in your marketing, the more people have access to you, which means the more opportunity they have to decide whether or not you are their cup of tea. This kind of polarization is a good thing. It is better that your prospective students realize quickly that you are not the teacher for them because this makes space for the students you do resonate with, and it allows you to refine your messaging based on their positive feedback. Remember, you don't need all the people; you need the right people—those who believe what you believe. Digital marketing also breeds haters because the method of communication is not direct. Folks are always more outspoken when they are not face-to-face.

Remember, you don't need all the people; you need the right people—those who believe what you believe.

Understand the difference between everyday content and professional content.

Yes, it is sexy to consider yourself a luxury brand and to want to have channels that are filled with highly polished, professional-quality content; I know I have lusted after a perfectly color-coordinated Instagram grid many times. However, my most successful clients have a nice mix of everyday content and professional content. A rule of thumb is 75 percent everyday content and 25 percent professional content.

Be genuine.

When building your audience, think about making real friends and connections, not just adding likes or followers. If you think about engaging with your audience as real people and seeking a way to be of service to them and add value for them, you will create a sense of authenticity that breeds growth.

Post often.

There is a direct relationship between account size and the number of posts. Large accounts post more often, so keep that in mind as you assess the overall health of your following. Here are my recommendations on the number of Facebook and Instagram posts per month based on the number of followers you have.

- Less than 999 followers: 7-8 posts per month
- Between 1,000 – 9,999 followers: 20-21 posts per month
- Between 10,000 – 99,999 followers: 41 Instagram and 47 Facebook posts per month
- Over 100,000 followers: 57 Instagram and 106 Facebook posts per month

Network with others.

In the same way that grassroots marketing connects networks in person, you can also connect and leverage networks online through cross-promotion, tagging and sharing, and other forms of online collaboration. When building your following online, don't be shy about looking for ways to work with others. People are more willing than you think to help you grow, plus they need to grow, too. One of the mechanisms of creating growth on social networks is based on the amount of sharing and mentions one has. You can grow by partnering with someone else who also wants to grow. Figure out fun ways to work together, and get to it. Some yoga teachers and studio owners even form pods where they commit to liking and commenting on each other's posts, which increases engagement for everyone.

Observe the give–sell ratio.

A rule of thumb for social media is to give 75 percent of the time and to sell 25 percent of the time. That means that three out of four posts are categorized as give. Take a peek at chapter 12 for a refresher on the relationship between what you give and what you sell.

Email Marketing: Newsletter Copy Best Practices

Building an email list and communicating with the people on the list regularly through newsletters is one of the most important marketing strategies you can leverage in your business. Of all of the marketing strategies, email marketing produces the highest conversion rate to sales. However, a lot of yoga teachers do not regularly collect email addresses, and they send their newsletters sporadically.

Planning ahead will help you keep your newsletters consistent. Plan your newsletter copy at least three months in advance, and be prepared to make shifts in the content if something has happened since you wrote it that affects the timeliness of your message or how it will be received (there's nothing worse than getting a prewritten newsletter that is tone deaf to the moment.). Starting your newsletters early will almost always ensure that they are sent on time. In chapter 16, we will build out your marketing schedule and there you can decide the frequency with which to send out your newsletter. A newsletter every week is ideal, but any pace which is consistent will be effective. Here is a list of components to include in your newsletters:

- *Subject line*—catchy and to the point
- *Header image*—fun, seasonal, timely
- *Intro*—personal words, thoughts, or inspiration from you
- *Free content*—a summary of your main "give"
- *Paid content*—a highlight of your main "sell" this month, including a link to the product or event on your website.
- *Press*—new highlights, updates, announcements, and partnerships
- *Footer image*—fun, seasonal, timely. Make sure your contact details are also visible here.

Use video.

Video use is directly linked to faster-growing channels of communication. The video doesn't need to be fancy or formal. The meteoric rise of TikTok shows just how powerful video content is. Consider ways that you can use video regularly on your channels. Nearly every message you can convey through text can also be conveyed by video. So if both methods take the same amount of work (many folks think video is faster), why not use the method that will naturally gain a larger response?

Engage with your followers.

Digital marketing should be a two-way conversation. A lot of yoga business owners have a one-way conversation with their followers, meaning they talk at and to their followers rather than talking with them. Yoga professionals with successful channels know that they need to get their people talking in order to grow. They ask questions of their followers and always respond to their answers in the comments.

It is my hope that after reading this chapter, you have a broader perspective of the digital marketing landscape and its role in our industry; the positive implications and enormous potential as well as the elements that are creating difficulty. I find it empowering to have a full understanding of an ecosystem when I participate in it and I hope that this chapter serves to do the same for you. In the next chapter, we will move on to event marketing, which is the most common marketing technique at work in the yoga space. Event marketing is the main vehicle by which all event-based service models are delivered.

15 EVENT MARKETING

Event marketing isn't typically considered a unique form of marketing, but it is so important to yoga business owners that I decided it is worthy of a chapter of its own. After all, getting students on yoga mats either in person or online is *the* goal of every yoga teacher and every yoga business. This makes having a firm understanding of what it takes to successfully market events vital to your success.

So, let's have a look at the essentials for successful marketing for events both in person and online. I will start with general concepts that apply to both in-person and online events, and then I will get specific on how best to market in each environment. I want you to be able to fill the room, time and time again.

ELEMENTS OF SUCCESSFUL EVENT MARKETING

The first element of successful event marketing is an early start. Almost everyone makes the mistake of beginning their promotions late because they failed to plan far enough ahead. This is why creating a marketing schedule and setting 24-month goals are essential to making things work in your business. The further ahead you can schedule your events and begin promoting them, the better the attendance at your events will be.

The first element of successful event marketing is an early start.

Many teachers fail to use the opportunities they have to promote an event when they are directly front of their students. Talk about your event and share your excitement. Your students are literally or virtually on the mat right in front of you—what an incredible opportunity to share with them your upcoming event! If you think back to how you ended up in a teacher training yourself, it was most likely because you heard a teacher you respect talking in class about an upcoming training. Think about the classes you teach like a TV show, with an opening segment and a closing segment, and consider how to use your time in those segments well. It may seem awkward to plug your next event at the beginning and end of the one you are currently leading, but the strongest marketers will tell you that these are juicy moments in which to promote yourself. At the beginning of class, your promotion joins a moment of excitement and anticipation. At the end of class, your promotion joins a moment of satisfaction because you have just delivered an incredible experience.

In-class promotion can be done gracefully in a way that is not obtrusive to the student's experience. When done consistently, it will provide you with a regular marketing opportunity for your events, and it will become commonplace for your students. They might even learn to love your promotions. I love many of the segments that begin and end my favorite shows.

Those of you who teach in a studio belonging to someone else may have a different reality when it comes to what you are allowed to say and do to promote your events in class. For events hosted at the studio or in partnership with the studio, in-class promotion is typically allowed. Promoting events that you are hosting without the studio's participation is typically not allowed, meaning you cannot promote events that are unassociated with the studio while you are in the studio. Even if the studio hasn't explicitly made a rule about this, I assure you that you do not want to be the teacher who is made an example of. Be sure to follow these rules to keep your relationship with your studios strong.

TYPES OF MARKETING MATERIALS FOR EVENTS

Marketing materials are the assets that you use to conduct your marketing through your communication channels. We will look at two types of marketing materials required for successful event marketing: Hard copy materials are physical pieces that you distribute by hand, and soft copy materials are digital pieces that you distribute online.

A set of well-designed marketing collateral to promote a particular event, such as an annual retreat or teacher training, includes hard and soft copy materials that share artwork specific to the event or series of events. Using similar artwork on all the materials that promote the event keeps your marketing schedule orderly and your communication channels tidy. And it helps people instantly recognize your event and makes it easier for them to take action and sign up. Can you imagine how distracting it would be to have a separate look for each piece of material promoting an event, not to mention confusing for your clients?

Hard Copy Marketing Materials

Hard copy marketing materials are physical materials that you distribute by hand or by mail or place at busy distribution points in your community. The five places you identified at the end of chapter 13 as great places to meet and connect with potential new clients are also great places to distribute your other hard copy marketing materials. Just make sure you ask for permission before leaving materials behind.

Real Talk

"I predicted that in five to ten years this poster will be well known . . . and it will be the beginning of a broad chance to contact a lot of people."
Dharma Mittra, on his legendary 908 yoga pose poster, arguably the most famous visual cue in the entire yoga space
Yoga teacher, practitioner, and guru of modern yoga

Having hard copy marketing materials on hand keeps you in the mindset of promoting. If everyone you need to know in order to make your dreams come true is already around you, you'd better make sure that you have something to give them. You can rock your grassroots marketing by leveraging your students' loyalty and giving them materials to give to other potential clients in their networks as well. In addition to being great for event marketing, consistent use of hard copy marketing materials is also great for general brand building because it creates another touch point and another layer of visibility for your business in the community.

Examples of hard copy marketing materials are listed here, although the possibilities are endless and as creative as you are:

Business cards

Postcards

Posters

Fliers

Pens and pencils

Matchbooks

Stickers

Stationery

Baseball caps

T-shirts

Tote bags

Make sure your hard copy materials include the basic vital details of your event:

- *Title*: What's the name of your event?
- *Date and time*: When and where will the event be held?
- *Description*: What should participants expect? What will they get? What will they experience? Why is this event important? Why should they spend money and time with you?
- *Contact and registration details*: How can people register for the event?
- *Price*: What is the investment participants need to make in order to attend the event?
- *Praise*: What have past attendees said or loved about your event? Include a few words of praise on your hard copy collateral. How many attended your event last time? Is space limited, or will it sell out? Be sure to include those details as well.

Soft Copy Marketing Materials

Soft copy marketing materials are the assets that you use to market your event through your online communication channels. Soft copy includes written text, images, and graphically designed pieces of artwork. For instance, if you will market your event on Facebook, you need a Facebook banner and a piece of artwork or an image for the Facebook ad. Or if you will engage in an email marketing campaign, you need to write the text for the email newsletter and collect images. Here are examples of soft copy marketing materials:

- *Website*—copy, images
- *Email marketing*—newsletter copy, images
- *E-commerce*—product descriptions, product images
- *YouTube*—copy, banner images, videos
- *Facebook*—copy, banner images, graphics for ads
- *Twitter*—copy, images, graphics for ads
- *Instagram*—copy, tiles, stories
- *Pinterest*—saved boards

YAMA Talent's free Airport Yoga Class Series with JetBlue.

BEST PRACTICES FOR EVENT MARKETING

It may seem that the possibilities for marketing an event and the communication channels to do so are endless, which can be overwhelming, but you can master them with practice and patience. Here are some of the things I've learned about how to effectively spend your time and maximize your event-marketing outreach.

Get grassroots.

Leverage your loyal network, and don't miss a beat connecting with a potential event attendee by having your hard copy marketing materials close at hand.

Tag and share.

In the same way that grassroots marketing allows you to activate someone else's network through a word-of-mouth connection and sharing, online event marketing also allows you to activate the network of someone else by tagging and sharing. You can expand the reach of your events by collaborating with your peers. When promoting your events online, feel free to tag friends and connections in the posts or ask them directly to share the event across their channels to help you promote. People are more willing than you think to help you achieve your dreams. You can offer them a discounted ticket to give away to their followers or some other kind of perk, including agreeing to promote an event of theirs across your channels when the time is right—sort of a "scratch my back, and I'll scratch yours" approach.

Be a storyteller.

With online event marketing, create posts about different elements of an event so that the copy for each post is unique (although all will include similar vital details). For instance, people respond well to "behind the scenes" content that lets them feel like they are part of the planning process to create the event, and getting insider access to what it takes to make the event a reality. Or you can post about why you created the event, what it means to you, and what the follower's support would mean to you if they attended. This kind of purpose-driven storytelling is compelling. It's as if you were personally inviting them to join your cause. There are so many elements of your event from start to finish that can be used to create interesting posts. Every bit of information is valuable, and you don't need to share a lot each time you post. The main point is to keep posting and to stay on everyone's radar.

Communicate often.

To effectively market your events, you need to communicate about your event frequently. Later in this section is a sample communication cadence along with sample language that you can use at each moment so that you can get a feel for the pace of the posts and the language that goes along with it. This is a minimum communication cadence. You can always share more often.

Many yogis are afraid to post frequently out of fear that they will overdo their marketing and lose clients who find it overly aggressive. Fear of overmarketing is unrealistic and keeps you from attaining the kind of consistency that successful marketing requires. Your students are busy and use multiple devices. The likelihood that they will see every one of your posts is slim to none. The *rule of seven* marketing adage tells us that it will take at least seven unique moments of communication before a student will buy from you—so you'd better get to it.

It is also worth noting that your students are used to being marketed to. Every day, thousands of brands and businesses vie for their attention and money, often promoting products that are detrimental to their health, so don't be afraid to make some noise and fight for your share of their attention and money. Just be sure to include the vital details listed earlier in the chapter each time you share. Lean into your content connection to keep your posts from becoming boring or redundant. Here is a sample communication cadence along with sample language.

> *Every day, thousands of brands and businesses vie for your students' attention and money, often promoting products that are detrimental to their health, so don't be afraid to make some noise and fight for your share of their attention and money.*

- *Share a save the date.* Post a save the date message the moment that you have secured a date for an event (e.g., Save the date! Annual alignment clinic in April!).
- *Share every other week from your save-the-date post up until 90 days before your event.* Post messages that tell your followers to join your event (e.g., Reserve your spot for my inaugural alignment clinic!).
- *Share once a week during the 90 days leading up to your event.* Post messages reminding your followers to join your event and create excitement for your event (e.g., Bring a friend. Treat yourself. There's still time to register. Only one spot left!).
- *Share twice a week before the start of your event.* Post a message that keeps the hype going and reminds your followers the event is coming up soon (e.g., See y'all next week at the alignment clinic!).

- *Share three days before the start of your event.* Post a message to generate excitement and let your followers know the day of the event is near (e.g., It's almost time for the alignment clinic!).
- *Share the day of the event.* Post a message telling your followers that the event is happening now, and as close to the event as you have time for given that you are also leading the event, share images and testimonials after the event (e.g., Alignment clinic starts today! Alignment clinic was amazing!).

Maintain an active calendar.

Event marketing benefits from having an accurate calendar of events accessible to attendees and potential attendees. It is important that your points of contact and communication channels include an up-to-date listing of your events and a one-click way to register. Keeping your schedule of events current is an ongoing task, but it is worth it. There's nothing worse than getting excited about a business and landing on their website to find a calendar that lists events that have already happened.

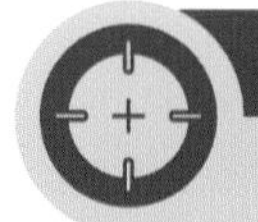

Your Yoga Business Homework

Observe Event Marketing

Being a great event marketer requires detailed planning and execution. I highly encourage exploring the marketing strategies of businesses in your hometown, like a favorite sports team or cultural institution, to gain inspiration from their event-marketing practices. For example, I receive the newsletter for the Brooklyn Nets basketball team. One of the most interesting things I noticed about their event marketing is that they sent out a "save the date" newsletter for the next season the very same night the Nets lost in the playoffs and their current season ended. That did not happen by accident. They wanted to get the save the date out as soon as possible, and they used the closing segment of their current season to do so. I also receive mail via post from the Nets, and any time I go to a game, I check out (and take home for design inspiration) an ample assortment of hard copy marketing materials. The Nets don't miss a moment to promote, and neither should you.

Choose two favorite out-of-industry businesses in your hometown, sign up for their mailing lists, and pay them a visit if they have a physical location. This will allow you to observe the full range of their event marketing practices and to see just how robust and creative their event-marketing practices are. Make a list of three to five notable characteristics of their event marketing that you love and can incorporate into your yoga business.

1. ______________________________
2. ______________________________
3. ______________________________
4. ______________________________
5. ______________________________

Getting students on yoga mats either in person or online is the goal of every yoga teacher and every yoga business. You've got to master the basics, keep yourself prepared with hard and soft copy collateral, and most importantly, stay consistent in order to make the most of things. Once you're in the groove of it, it becomes second nature. Many of us first experienced event marketing as the result of communications directed at us by our very first yoga teacher—though we probably didn't even realize we were being marketed to! And that's sort of the point. In the following chapter, we will put all the pieces of your marketing strategy together and help you get organized!

16 YOUR MARKETING SCHEDULE

My cousin Deanna is a high-profile art designer at a big-name media outlet in New York City. I love to grab a meal with her when she can fit me in her schedule and hear all about her high-rise escapades with her huge teams, huge deliverables, and huge deadlines—you know, the behind-the-scenes, "making of the magic" type stuff! I often ask questions about the operating infrastructure because that's the kind of nerd I am. What I find to be most interesting (totally surprising!) is how simple some of the tools are that are used to run these complex organizations, where a lot of detail is involved and tremendous consistency is required. I mean, there's nothing more pressing than if you have to deliver a complete newspaper every day or magazine every month. A simple tool used well is not to be underestimated. A simple tool holds in its simplicity the likelihood that you will use it to create a great product (in our case, amazing marketing) on a regular basis.

The heart of successful marketing is simplicity, consistency, and organization. They allow you to commit to your marketing as if you were a big-name magazine and had the whole world waiting impatiently for your news or information to come hot off the press. So let's take a look at a simple tool with big potential: your marketing schedule, which is one of our favorite ways to stay organized.

UNDERSTANDING YOUR MARKETING SCHEDULE

An effective marketing schedule houses a concise marketing plan and permits you to own your marketing rather than being overwhelmed by it by allowing you to plan ahead, stay ahead, and remember information that is essential to communicate as you make your way through the calendar year. The marketing schedule also allows you to manage and maximize all of your marketing responsibilities from one central location. I've provided a five-month example of a marketing schedule in figure 16.1 so you can see what I mean. But first, let's take a look at how your marketing schedule will be organized.

The horizontal columns of your marketing schedule include the following:

- *Communication channel*: This column lists your various communications channels, such as hard copy, events, digital platforms, and other communications such as e-commerce, paid advertising, email, newsletters, and your evergreen goods, services, and events.
- *Frequency per month*: This column tracks how often you aim to post on the channel each month. This will help remind you of your overall posting commitments.
- *Focus of the month*: This column is where you choose which of your goods, services, and events you will focus on communicating about for the month. Your focus of the month will be a mix of your upcoming events and your goods and services that you constantly market, such as your one-to-one sessions.
- *Production required*: This column details production needs for an upcoming focus of the month. It takes time to create content and develop marketing assets such as designing hard copy collateral or hosting a photo shoot; therefore, it is important to realistically estimate what is required to produce marketing assets well in advance of when you will need to distribute them.

Your marketing schedule is then organized vertically by listing your evergreen goods and services, your events (special, cyclical, and personal), digital marketing channels, and other communication channels that you use to market your yoga business. Let's take a closer look:

Evergreen Goods and Services

Within every business, there are evergreen goods and services to be marketed. Evergreen refers to the fact that these goods and services are enduring items on your menu of services. Evergreen goods and services are those that you consistently market and sell. You only need to look as far as your favorite clothing store to understand what I mean. Yes, there will be special in-store events, holiday sales, and anniversary events that will be marketed throughout the year, but even on a regular day, your favorite clothing store is selling products. It's the same for your yoga business, and it is important that you do not lose sight of the need to market enduring and regularly scheduled events or products such as your weekly classes or one-to-one packages. You want to make sure that your evergreen products as well as your special events and offers are well scheduled on the marketing schedule!

Events

- *Special events and product launches*: These are the special events or products that you will sell during the year and that you will communicate about frequently in the months leading up to these special events and launches. The easiest way to properly market these is to work backward by placing the date of your event or product launch onto the marketing schedule first and then working your marketing strategy backward to build in what you want to do to promote the event or launch between now and then. For example, if deposits are due November 1 for a training that begins January 1, you will place January 1 as the training launch, November 1 deposits due, and May 1 as a save the date. Your marketing schedule will need to consistently communicate and encourage registration from May to November. All important special events and program or product launch dates should be on the schedule with as much lead time as possible.
- *Cyclical events*: These are opportunities to align your sales and marketing with holidays and seasonal changes in the calendar that create exciting marketing moments of communication throughout the year. Cyclical events are great ways to organize content and keep your marketing timely, fresh, and exciting. For instance, making sure you have an offer during Black Friday or Women's Empowerment Month or to celebrate the summer solstice are all great ways to capitalize on cyclical events. There are lots of cyclical events, and you do not need to hit them all; however, keeping cyclical events top of mind is a smart way to plan your year in advance and to always be in tune with the market.
- *Personal events*: These are opportunities such as birthdays and anniversaries (either work or personal in nature) that you can tap into to create exciting marketing moments of communication throughout the year. For example, I often make a point to note YAMA's birthday each year in January and use it as an opportunity to tell the story about how YAMA came to be and, of course, to run a sale on one of my yoga services to celebrate.

Digital Marketing Channels

As covered in depth in chapter 14, your digital marketing channels include all of your online-based communications. A well-designed marketing schedule will include efforts to communicate an event or product launch across all of your chosen communication channels. As we discussed in chapter 15 about the rule of seven (it will take at least seven unique moments of communication before a student will take action), you need to communicate often across all of your channels, and it's unlikely your clients will see every one of your messages. So if you market on Instagram, you also need to market via email, on your website, via word of mouth, and so on. To the greatest extent possible, each evergreen good and service and each special event and product launch should be marketed across the majority of your communication channels. For instance, if you are only marketing your weekly classes on Twitter, you are missing out on marketing to the audiences on all your other communication channels.

Your Yoga Business Homework

Create Your Marketing Schedule

In this activity, you are going to create your own marketing schedule. To begin, download the marketing schedule template from HK*Propel* (instructions are provided at the front of this book). Next, fill in your horizontal and vertical headers to complete a 13-month schedule running from December to January. It's great to start with the last month of the year because, as mentioned, you will likely have marketing materials that need to be produced the month before the marketing plan begins. Your vertical list of communication channels should only include the channels that you are actively using in your business.

Starting at the top of your marketing schedule, place your evergreen goods and services that are to be consistently marketed in your business. (Skip hard copy for now!) Then, fill in all of your events, remembering to place all your special events and product launches on the calendar on the date they occur and work backward to add important dates such as registration deadlines. From here, pause, sit back, and take a look at the upcoming three months of goods and services that you need to market. Ask yourself how you will market them. Refer to the marketing channels, techniques, and strategies that we learned about in chapters 13, 14, and 15. There are endless possibilities! Then, finally, complete your marketing schedule to the best of your ability for the entire year.

The marketing schedule becomes your go-to resource for what to share and when. Once the marketing schedule is complete for the year, print out a few months of the schedule at a time and hang it on the wall so that you can see in front of you what you've already completed and what is coming. The visual reminder works wonders to keep the important dates top of mind. I have clients who use a whiteboard marketing schedule that covers an entire wall of their home office to stay organized and excited about their marketing.

Available online on HK*Propel*.

FIGURE 16.1 Sample Five-Month Marketing Schedule

Communication channel		Frequency per month	December		January		February		March		April	
			Focus of the month	Production required	Focus of the month	Production required	Focus of the month	Production required	Focus of the month	Production required	Focus of the month	Production required
Evergreen goods and services			*One-to-one packages*		*Weekly online class*							
Events	Special events, product launches			*Create hard copy for alignment clinic*		*Drop alignment clinic hard copy at five locations*					*Alignment clinic*	
	Cyclical events				*New Year*		*Valentine's Day*		*Women's Empowerment Month; summer solstice*			
	Personal events											
Digital marketing channels	Website											

(continued)

FIGURE 16.1 Sample Five-Month Marketing Schedule *(continued)*

Communication channel	Frequency per month	December		January		February		March		April	
		Focus of the month	Production required	Focus of the month	Production required	Focus of the month	Production required	Focus of the month	Production required	Focus of the month	Production required
YouTube				Reserve your spot for my alignment clinic		Treat yourself this Valentine's Day to my alignment clinic (10% savings all weekend)					
Vimeo											
Facebook											
Twitter			Create artwork for alignment clinic	Reserve your spot for my alignment clinic		Treat yourself this Valentine's Day to my alignment clinic (10% savings all weekend)		See you next month at the alignment clinic!			

Communication channel	Frequency per month	December		January		February		March		April	
		Focus of the month	Production required	Focus of the month	Production required	Focus of the month	Production required	Focus of the month	Production required	Focus of the month	Production required
Instagram			Create artwork for alignment clinic	Reserve your spot for my alignment clinic		Treat yourself this Valentine's Day to my alignment clinic (10% savings all weekend)	Special guest for March IG live	IG live: Importance of good alignment with special guest			
Snapchat											
Pinterest			Create artwork for alignment clinic	Reserve your spot for my alignment clinic		Treat yourself this Valentine's Day to my alignment clinic (10% savings					
TikTok											
LinkedIn											

(continued)

FIGURE 16.1 Sample Five-Month Marketing Schedule *(continued)*

Communication channel		Frequency per month	December		January		February		March		April	
			Focus of the month	Production required	Focus of the month	Production required	Focus of the month	Production required	Focus of the month	Production required	Focus of the month	Production required
Other	Blogging and vlogging		Write an article on the importance of good alignment		Post article to website; distribute via newsletter and social media							
	Email											
	Newsletter			Create artwork for alignment clinic	Reserve your spot for my alignment clinic		Treat yourself this Valentine's Day to my alignment clinic (10% savings					
	Podcast											
	Text											
	SEO											

Communication channel	Frequency per month	December		January		February		March		April	
		Focus of the month	Production required	Focus of the month	Production required	Focus of the month	Production required	Focus of the month	Production required	Focus of the month	Production required
Paid advertising				Run ad for alignment clinic: Reserve your spot for the alignment clinic now!		Run ad for alignment clinic: Treat yourself to my alignment clinic this Valentine's Day (enjoy 10% savings all weekend)					
E-commerce		End-of-the-year sale (50% off all online products)	Link to alignment clinic	Alignment clinic on website home page							

ORGANIZING YOUR MARKETING MATERIALS

How and where will you keep and store all of the amazing marketing materials that you are producing to bring your marketing plan to life? A key to being able to work through and build out your marketing schedule quickly and effectively is being well organized and having a logical filing system for all of your marketing materials.

This filing system will be your one-stop shop, where you can "grab and go" for all of your marketing needs, and it provides a way to smartly store your library of assets for use and repurposing. The task of creating a system that works for you can be a bit labor intensive, especially for people who have been in business for a while and have not been organizing their assets well. But I assure you that taking the time to do so will help you move faster across your marketing objectives in the long run.

Here's what works well for me. I have a master folder named Marketing Assets, in a location that I can easily access from all of my devices, including my phone. Google Drive and Dropbox are both storage systems I love. Within this master folder, I create subfolders by year, and then within each year's subfolder, I have folders for hard copy, soft copy, press, and inspiration.

Right on, y'all. We have now completed part IV, Refine Your Message! You've done such exciting and gorgeous work and are truly ready to put your message on a mission. In the next part, we will work on creating connections to support you in achieving your 24-month goals.

PART V
WORK YOUR PLAN

17
CREATE CONNECTIONS

I'm not sure in what mythical fairy-tale world the doorbell rings and everything you've ever wanted is standing on the other side when you open the door, but for some reason this is how many yoga professionals tend to think about how they will obtain the business of their dreams!

> *I have great goals and great dreams, and I'm amazing! Now, I think I'll sit around and wait for someone to bring my dreams to me on a silver platter.*

Unfortunately, this will not happen, and you will have to go after those great goals and great dreams yourself. It's terrifying and empowering at the same time to know that everything you dream of is possible if you create the opportunities for yourself. And why not go for it? You never know what you can get unless you ask. You never know what's possible until you try. As cliche as it sounds, it's the truth. There are a lot fewer people going for it than you would think because many people spend their whole lives waiting for the doorbell of opportunity to ring. I am not saying that creating opportunity for yourself is easy. And it is an art form. It requires developing a thick skin and determination. But what could be more worth it than to go after your dreams? Even if you don't achieve them all, the journey of going toward those dreams is fulfilling and often quite profitable.

It was difficult for me to choose which story about creating opportunity to share with you because I've dreamed about a million dreams, and I've gone after most of them. This is mainly because I stand in my purpose, *and* because I know just how few people go after their dreams, which makes my chances of getting through pretty good.

Speaking of going after your dreams . . . I've cold-called Oprah Winfrey's office, DM'd major celebrities, done pop-up stunts in the middle of Times Square, sent emails every day to a decision maker until getting a call back, landed exclusive magazine covers and endorsements, produced the first yoga reality TV show and the world's largest yoga classes, and created partnerships with A-list brands by walking in off the street. Heck, I even pitched myself for this book deal. The concept of creating opportunity is the same whether your dreams are to be an exceptional hobby teacher, a regional rock star, or a household name because, simply put, these dreams will not come to you. You'll need to pick up the phone, pitch yourself, ask for the business, and do the follow-up because opportunity doesn't knock; you do.

Opportunity doesn't knock; you do.

In this chapter we will review my tried-and-true tools, techniques, and best practices for creating opportunity:

- Creating a great elevator introduction
- Mastering the partnership pitch
- Crafting an effective partnership letter or direct message
- Adopting best practices for successful networking
- Identifying potential partners

Real Talk

"At numerous points in my professional career, something has happened and we've seized the opportunity, and many other things have sprung off of that, which allowed us to ride a wave of momentum. And when that wave dips, rather than being upset at the dip, it's a time to conserve—to focus on your home base and then get ready for the next opportunity, which I know is coming, so that when it comes, you're pouring from a full cup with energy and with drive."
Finlay Wilson
Founder of Heart Space, a yoga not-for-profit, and creator of Kilted Yoga

CRAFTING YOUR ELEVATOR INTRODUCTION

Because the name of our game is to be able to use each and every opportunity to create connections to promote your yoga business, you will need to have materials ready for each type of circumstance you will find yourself in, which is why having a solid elevator introduction is so important. When someone asks you what you do, it's likely that you won't have a lot of time to answer. As a resident of New York City, I use my elevator intro (or hear someone else's) at least two or three times a day. It's part of our interconnected lifestyle here and the reality that we all depend on each other. Regardless of where you live, it's great practice to be able to succinctly explain your work to someone in less time than it would take to ride in an elevator together.

A great elevator introduction takes less than 30 seconds and includes the why, how, and what of your yoga business and then one last piece, the attention-grabbing part of your elevator pitch—the glitter as it were. When you're moving fast, you want to get right to it, so consider dropping the poetic language. And you get bonus points if you add something exciting or attention grabbing.

For instance, here is my purpose statement:

> I am a catalyst for better living and bring the tools of wellness to communities of all kinds. I serve my mission daily by providing guidance, tools, and infrastructure to a diverse roster of clients in the wellness space.

But my elevator introduction looks like this:

> I am a biz manager for yoga teachers (what), and my goal is to bring the tools of wellness to communities of all kinds (why). I serve my mission daily by providing artist representation and strategic advising services (how) to a diverse roster of clients in the wellness space. They call me the Ari Gold of yoga! (attention grabber)

Your Yoga Business Homework

Write Your Elevator Introduction

Refer back to your purpose statement in chapter 1. Make edits to your purpose statement to make it more conversational and crystal clear. Use the prompts and write out all four elements of your elevator introduction—why, what, how, and an attention grabber.

Why: ______________________________

What: ______________________________

How: ______________________________

Attention grabber: ______________________________

Now, write your complete elevator introduction:

____

____

____

____

____

____

____

Once you have written your complete elevator introduction, practice it aloud with a timer—like for real. You are shooting for 30 seconds max. Most of us don't memorize our elevator pitches verbatim and state it robotically when we meet someone. But most of life happens in impromptu moments, so having these four key elements in your pocket will ensure that you are confident in introducing your business or at least saying *something* about it when you're in the elevator.

CREATING YOUR PARTNERSHIP PITCH

The partnership pitch is a more formal method of creating connections and promoting a yoga business that I use regularly. I love pitching at the end or beginning of the year to all of my existing contacts and to some new folks that I'd love to work with on new business opportunities. It's important for the longevity of your business that your business stays top of mind with your business contacts; the squeaky wheel really does get the oil, and being in the right place at the right time doesn't happen by accident. The partnership pitch will empower you to connect with yoga studios, brands, and media regularly. As my daddy used to say, "Sometimes you gotta throw the noodles on the wall until they stick!"

In this section, we will explore the key components of a great partnership pitch, how to speak to the people you are reaching out to in business terms that they value and recognize, the importance of adding value, and how to create a clearly outlined proposal. First up, let's break down the key components of your pitch. Each element conveys an important part of your story, allows the recipient to get to know you, and creates a foundation of trust. All of which sets you up to clearly present the business opportunity you are pitching.

- *Write a warm and personal introduction.* No one wants to feel like they're getting bulk mail. So in addition to using the person's name, include a connection that you have with the outlet you are pitching. Taking the time to make this connection shows effort, and that effort forms the basis of a strong relationship.
- *Include a friendly image of yourself making eye contact.* Choosing to go into business with someone is a form of relationship. And most of us want to see the face of the person we are going to be in a relationship with, so I highly recommend including an image of yourself with your pitch. The photo does not need to be a pricey professional headshot—a candid, energetic photo from your cell phone will also do.
- *Share your purpose.* As you have learned, you want to lead with your purpose as often as possible. Be sure to include all or part of your purpose statement from chapter 1.
- *Share some of your experience and your expertise.* Highlights from your resume are important when soliciting new business opportunities. Also choose one or two key elements from your remarkable bio.
- *Share a little bit of your success.* No one wants to be the first to book you or to collaborate with you. Sharing one or two key accomplishments is paramount in getting the next opportunity.
- *Clarify the ask.* Often we connect with people we would like to collaborate with, but we do not tell them exactly how we can be of service or how we can add value to their business. How can you help the yoga studio, brand, or media outlet? Tell them explicitly, and give them an example of how good your work is or a testimonial of what others have said about your work.
- *Provide a clear follow-up window.* It will help you stick to your follow-up plan if you declare that you will follow up. Plus, it's great for building trust in a potential business partner when you do what you say you are going to do.

Take a look at the sample pitch letter in figure 17.1. This sample incorporates all of the key elements of a great pitch.

Because social media has increased the number of communication channels that exist between a business, the market, and its partners, there are new ways to pitch yourself, the most popular of which is direct messaging. If you haven't ever "slid into someone's DMs" to make a business connection, get ready.

Like it or not (I did not like it!) and believe it or not (I did not want to believe it!), direct messaging (DM) on social media is an effective way to create new connections. Use direct messaging to complement your email outreach; it is not effective when used alone. It may be sufficient on its own when you are creating connections with other yoga teachers, but even then, I suggest a multipronged approach to creating new connections. A great partnership DM will include the details of your elevator introduction and include a clear proposal for how you would like to collaborate.

FIGURE 17.1 Sample Pitch Letter

Hi, *[Insert Person's Name Here]*,

Warm and personal introduction

I hope this email finds you well and reflective as you prepare for the new year; I know I am. It's an honor to meet you, and I absolutely love the work you do at *[insert studio name here]*.

Share your purpose

My name is Ava Taylor, and my mission is to be a catalyst for better living and to bring the tools of wellness to communities of all kinds. I have served my mission daily since 2009 by providing guidance, tools, and infrastructure to a diverse roster of clients in the wellness space through my company, YAMA Talent.

Friendly image of yourself making eye contact

Share some of your experience, expertise, and success

I am an agent, author, and small-business coach and a CEU provider with the Yoga Alliance. I was recently featured in an article, "Catalyst for Success," by *Fitness Business Insider* and produced and headlined an online business summit for yoga teachers called INSPIRE. For a full bio, recent press, appearances, and testimonials, please visit my website: yamatalent.com.

I am a tenacious entrepreneur, an avid yogi, and a sought-out media contributor and speaker known for having my finger on the pulse of the rapidly expanding yoga industry. I'm also the creator of The Catalyst online business school for yogis and author of *Your Yoga Business*, published by Human Kinetics.

Clarify the ask

I would love to lead a workshop or lecture at *[insert studio name here]* and have attached a list of topics for your review. Here's a testimonial from my last workshop: "The Catalyst is my secret weapon. Ava's content is highly recommended!" I can appear at *[insert studio name here]* either in person or online.

Please let me know if you would be interested in collaborating! I am sure I can create an exciting and revenue-generating event at *[insert studio name here]*.

I look forward to hearing back from you and will follow up this same time next week.

Provide a clear follow-up window

In health,

Ava Taylor

PS: Feel free to keep in touch online as well! @yamatalent @avantaylor

FIGURE 17.2 Sample Direct Message

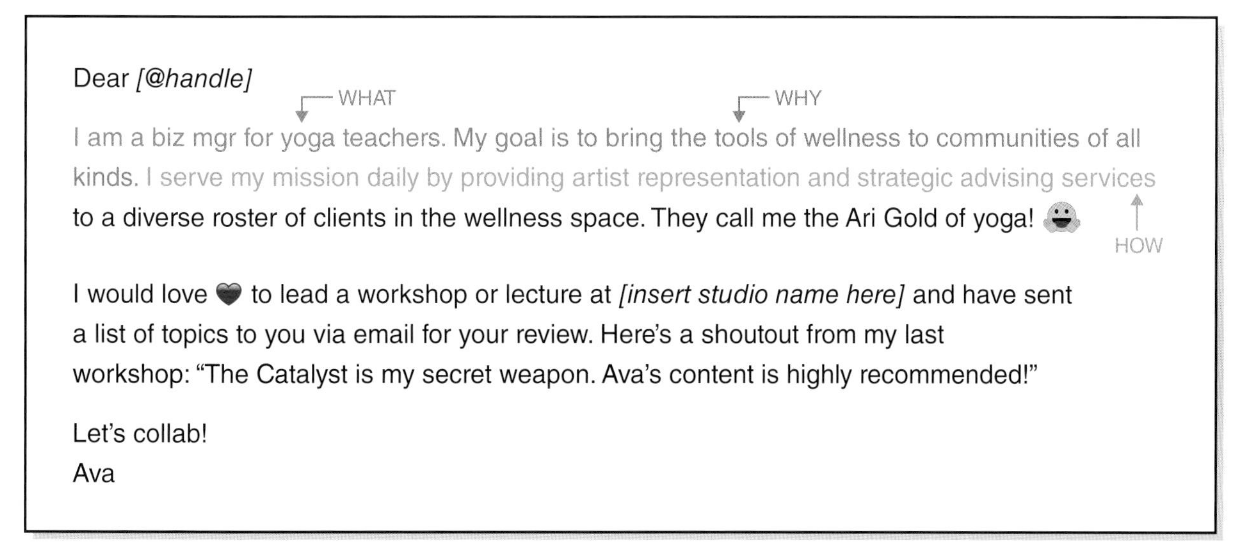

Dear *[@handle]*

I am a biz mgr for yoga teachers. My goal is to bring the tools of wellness to communities of all kinds. I serve my mission daily by providing artist representation and strategic advising services to a diverse roster of clients in the wellness space. They call me the Ari Gold of yoga!

I would love to lead a workshop or lecture at *[insert studio name here]* and have sent a list of topics to you via email for your review. Here's a shoutout from my last workshop: "The Catalyst is my secret weapon. Ava's content is highly recommended!"

Let's collab!
Ava

Feel free to abbreviate and use emojis to shorten the text and make the DM stand out. Take a look at figure 17.2 for an example of a great direct message.

Before we finish this section, I'd like to address two of the issues that often keep yoga business owners from being successful in pitching their ideas. Don't let these happen to you!

1. *Fear of rejection*. Most yogis stop before they start when it comes to increasing opportunities for themselves because of a fear of rejection. The reality is that increasing opportunities for yourself is a numbers game: You have to knock on a lot of doors before one will open to you. Therefore, there's a natural amount of rejection that is simply part of the game. No one bats 1,000. If you understand this and don't take it personally when people say no or don't respond, you'll have a much easier time putting yourself out there. Speaking of knocking on a lot of doors, take a look at the next issue.
2. *Not following up*. Most yoga teachers think their job is done when they send the first email or direct message. (Yoga teacher pats self on the back, and says, "Yay, I did it!") People are busy, and the world is noisy, so there is no guarantee that your first message reached its target. I typically follow up after seven business days, then again, and again until I get a response, even if it's a no. Getting a no from an important business can be considered a huge win. A no means that you successfully reached your target and that your name is now in their ecosystem. After three follow-up attempts, I typically move on until I have fresh news to share or a new way to add value to their business.

Your Yoga Business Homework
Write Your Pitch Letter or Direct Message

Now it's your turn to draft a pitch letter and a direct message. Use the key components of your pitch and the following prompts to begin crafting the components of your letter or DM:

Write a warm and personal introduction: ______________________________

____

Write your purpose statement: ______________________________

____

Write one or two key elements from your remarkable bio: ______________________________

____

Write one or two key accomplishments: ______________________________

____

Write the ask: ______________________________

____

Write how and when you will follow up: ______________________________

____

LEVERAGING YOUR NETWORK

I often refer to the business of yoga as the Wild West because there are so many opportunities to create; I truly believe they're endless. And if we have learned anything together throughout the course of this book, it is that the success of your yoga business is almost entirely up to you. Some yoga business owners find this fact intimidating, while others find it inspiring. I find it inspiring because I love knowing that there isn't anyone or anything standing in the way of my clients or me achieving our goals!

What if I said that the key to making your dreams come true wasn't found at the bottom of the ocean or at the top of an impossibly high mountain, but rather in the desk drawer of your neighbor's house? What if Oprah isn't the only person who can make your dreams come true? (Don't tell her I said that!) What if the person who always says hello to you at your local coffee shop, an old friend from high school, or even one of your existing students holds the key to your dreams?

The success of your yoga business is almost entirely up to you.

It might seem unbelievable that everyone you need to know to make your dreams come true is already around you, but I know that it is true from having watched it happen time and time again. I also know that this way of thinking helps you to properly mine your existing network and relationships, which helps to amplify your business and propel it to the next level!

Yes, there are big breaks, and yes, sometimes we get lucky, and a door will magically swing open, and a high-profile person will reach through, take our hand, and show us to the top. And yes, sometimes we even get to Oprah—but the momentum you need to reach the next stage of your business doesn't rely on people you don't already have access to, and it sure doesn't rely on getting lucky. The majority of successful yoga business owners will agree. It's what I call a ground-up and top-down approach. When you are invested in your own dreams and mission on the ground level, you will find that you can use your own network to reach amazing new heights.

It's kind of like when former President Barack Obama speaks about the government and how people typically focus every four years on high-level national elections even when there is real work, change, and opportunity happening on a grassroots level right here in your own neighborhood every single day. Believing that you can level up by activating the network of people you already know is a radical new way to think about growing your business. It means that nothing is standing in the way of your success. What would happen if you connected to, communicated with, and engaged those around you in the pursuit of your dreams, their dreams, and your common goals?

Keep Oprah on your wish list, but work the ground-up angle, too. When you are employing all of your resources on the ground level, the universe will reciprocate, and those high-profile connections will eventually follow. So let's get to work on properly activating your network using a strategy I call *leveraging*.

To leverage means to use something to its maximum advantage, and in our case, that something refers to your relationships—those with people you already know and relationships that you want to cultivate. Maximizing your relationships is a vital part of your yoga business, and when used properly, can create more opportunity and more incentive for others to support you in becoming your dreams. In the following exercises, you will learn skills and strategies for effectively creating leverage.

Networking Matters

I make it my business to attend a networking event either in person or online at least once a month—and it doesn't need to be a formal networking event. Taking a class at a new studio or attending the lecture or workshop of a peer or someone whose name is new to you are great chances to meet potential new clients and collaborators, and they keep the creative juices flowing. They also allow you to stay visible in the community. You would be surprised how many opportunities go to people who are simply present. It's the opposite of out of sight, out of mind.

Remember when leveraging and networking to ask how you can help others achieve their goals; it is vital to know what their dreams are as well. Find out how you can add value. I have fantastic networkers (extremely successful business owners) in my community, and the first thing they will ask me after we have exchanged formalities is, "What are you working on, and how can I help?"

Most of us have far more to offer than we think that can support those who can support us in leveling up. You will only find out what they need if you are willing to open up the conversation. It's one thing to meet someone. It's another to meet them, to find out how you can mutually support each other, and then to follow through on it.

Let Me Repeat It: Follow Up

Just as important as following up on your formal pitches is to get back in touch with people you meet. Some of us go through the effort to network and meet new people and then do not follow up. I have had new clients turn over stacks and stacks of business cards or heaps of scrap paper with contact details on them of people that they met and never followed up with. If you put in the effort to make contact, finish the job! Save their information on a contact list or in an app, and do the work of actually connecting with them—even if the outreach is just to say, "It was wonderful to meet you, and I look forward to circling back about opportunities to collaborate."

Also, know that it is never too late to follow up. I have had great success creating connections with old contacts whether I am rekindling or initiating the relationship. I once had a client who had been offered a radio interview three years earlier. She mentioned it to me with dismay that even though she had been generously offered the interview, she was too shy to follow up. I encouraged her to see if her contact was still there and to ask if the interview opportunity was still available. Sure enough, her contact was still there and was so thrilled to finally hear from her that not only did she get an interview, she got a series of them. Usually people who say they want to help you achieve your goals are genuine about it—so don't be shy about taking them up on their offer.

Parlay Your Value

When working on maximizing your relationships, it is important to keep people in the know about your continued growth and success. As your business grows, your value increases, and you want to make sure that everyone you know knows about it. For example, if you have a studio you're trying to host a workshop at, you can take a testimonial from a student or a video clip of yourself teaching the workshop at another venue and share it with the studio owner of the location you are trying to get into. Or perhaps you want to teach at a conference or festival and receive a great piece of press from a media outlet; you can use that press hit to knock on the door and introduce yourself or follow up with the conference or festival. It is especially important to regularly follow up with media outlets, brands, and contacts that are on your dream list. But don't knock on the door with the same old information; knock with news of accomplishments, growth, and new ideas for content.

By parlaying, you can use your current wins to set up your next move until you get that dream contact to pay attention to you! Even getting a no from a dream contact can be considered a success. After all, a response is an acknowledgment that they know who you are. It is also important to connect directly where possible with those on your hot list (we'll learn about this in the next section). Attending their events in person or online shows them your support and gives you something to talk to them about. I have a rule to participate in the business of a contact before creating a connection—for example, by taking a class or buying a copy of their book. This puts me in a favorable position for beginning a relationship. Being good at parlaying allows you to be persistent without being a pest. Most people want you to achieve your dreams just as much as they want to achieve their own. It is your job to give them the chance and to return the favor.

© Meghan Powell

I love this snap of yogi and friend Keith Mitchell at the White House Easter Egg Roll. Most of the people you need to make your dreams come true are already around you.

IDENTIFYING YOUR HOT LIST

Now that you've learned how to create pitches and how to use connections to your advantage, it's time to build the list of contacts that you will send your pitches to. I call this your *hot list*.

As I have said before, most of the people you need to make your dreams come true are already around you—so your hot list will be one part existing contacts for potential collaboration and one part aspirational contacts for potential collaboration.

Even if I am not actively pitching my hot list on a business opportunity, I like to update and check in with the contacts on my list at least once a year. People in business are used to this kind of connection, and it helps to build your reputation as a true business owner when people see that you are keeping your contact list up to date. Folks on your existing contact list may have gotten a new job somewhere you are interested in working, traveled somewhere you are interested in going, or met someone you are interested in meeting. The only way to assess their ability to help you is to regularly engage with them. So many times I have experienced an old contact becoming new again. It is vital that you offer to support them as well—but in short, offering support and providing it where appropriate can create a kind of currency that can be exchanged later.

Your Yoga Business Homework

Create Your Hot List and Start Pitching

Let's start by creating a spreadsheet that lists all of your existing and aspirational contacts including collaborators, media outlets, and brands. Then, research each one so that you can gather a complete set of contact details, such as email addresses, phone numbers, website addresses, and social media handles. Try not to feel that someone on your aspirational list is unreachable. I once tried every email format and syntax at Oprah's office at Harpo Studios until I got through to someone at the office, so I feel pretty confident saying that if you *really* want to reach someone, you can. I usually look for someone in community for talent partnerships or new business development. A few minutes of research online usually will get you to the right person or to someone who will be able to direct you to the right person.

Next, add columns to your spreadsheet for tracking the dates you contact each person and for notes with the answers to these questions:

- How can they help my business level up?
- How can I help them level up?
- What can I parlay to get them to take notice of me?

Once you have completed the spreadsheet of your hot list, send a pitch letter or DM to 10 of the contacts on your hot list.

Available online on HK*Propel*.

As you can see, from all we have covered in this chapter, opportunity is literally everywhere around you. With intention, thoughtfulness, preparation, courage, and consistency, you can create an enormous amount of momentum and new opportunity for your yoga business.

18
IDENTIFY STRATEGIES

Earlier in the book, we established that great accomplishments start with great dreams, and we learned that becoming your dream is the result of three stages:

1. The place where we begin
2. The choosing of our destination
3. The effort to arrive

Previous chapters discussed the first two stages. We will now explore the third stage: the effort required to get where you are going. You have taken a great step toward becoming your dream by clearly defining what you want. Your dreams now ask of you, and I now ask of you, to start to take action toward making your dreams a reality. Achieving your dream goals depend on implementing great strategies, such as setting midpoint goals and identifying what we call bridge strategies. Are you willing to put in the effort to make your dreams come true? The answer must be yes!

In chapter 10, you assessed your starting point, and in chapter 11, you chose your dream goals and set SMART 24-month goals. You will now identify your 12-month midpoint goals as well as the bridge strategies that will take you from your starting point to your 12-month midpoint goals and from your 12-month midpoint goals to your 24-month goals. Both your 12- and 24-month goals are midpoint goals that describe what you need to achieve on your way to your dream goals, and the bridge strategies are literally how you will achieve them.

Your goals are only as good as the strategies you implement to achieve them.

SET MIDPOINT GOALS

Your 12-month goals should be reasonably placed between your starting point and your final destination. These goals can be a good way to check how realistic the timing of your goals is. If, when you walk backward from the 24-month goal, you find that you cannot make a reasonable 12-month goal, then you may have set an unrealistic 24-month goal. This doesn't mean that your dream goal has to change, but rather that you need to adjust the timeframe for meeting your dream goal.

For example, if your dream goal is to become a full-time teacher earning $150,000 a year in six years, then the 24-month goal is to achieve $80,000. A reasonable 12-month midpoint goal would be to achieve $60,000, which is a $25,000 increase over your starting point income of $35,000. On the other hand, if you set your dream goal to reach $150,000 a year in three years, then your 24-month goal would need to be $115,000, which is a pretty steep increase from $35,000 in two years. Take a look at figure 18.1 for an example of 12-month midpoint goals, which build toward the 24-month midpoint goals and the dream goals.

FIGURE 18.1 Sample Build Your Dreams Worksheet: 12-Month Midpoint Goals

Service model	12-month goal	24-month goal	Dream goal	By when?
One-to-one sessions	Sell 40 private sessions at $125 per session	Sell 100 private sessions at $150 per session	Earn $25,000 per year	6 years
Group sessions	Add one additional weekly class	Increase revenue	Earn $50,000 per year	6 years
Conferences and festivals	Build solid relationships with conference or festival producers; build list of 10 local and regional conferences or festivals and contacts for booking	Pitch myself to 10 conferences or festivals	Teach at two conferences or festivals per year and earn $5,000	6 years
Workshops	Create and lead a series of in-person workshops	Sell two weekend workshops per year	Travel four times a year to lead workshops and earn $10,000	24 months
Immersions				
Retreats	Find both a regional and international location and run a sample budget for each in the tour calculator	Run my first regional retreat with at least eight participants	Host one retreat and have one week vacation each year and earn $12,500	24 months
Trainings	Begin a 300-hour training program	Complete 300- hour training program	Become a teacher trainer with 20 graduates per year and earn $35,000	10 years
Products and merchandise	Write the table of contents and first chapter of my book	Complete the manuscript for my book	Become a published author	6 years
	Complete my favorite brands list; grow my email list to 1,500	Grow my email list to 3,000	Secure a paid ambassador relationship with one of my favorite brands; email list of 10,000	6 years

Your Yoga Business Homework

Set Midpoint Goals

Refer to your build your dreams worksheet in chapter 11 (see figure 11.3 on page 120). Now, in figure 18.2, you will add realistic 12-month midpoint goals for each of your service models to support the achievement of your 24-month goals.

FIGURE 18.2 Build Your Dreams Worksheet: 12-Month Midpoint Goals

Service model	12-month goal	24-month goal	Dream goal	By when?
One-to-one sessions				
Group sessions				
Conferences and festivals				
Workshops				
Immersions				
Retreats				
Trainings				
Products and merchandise				

To help you further understand how your 12-month goals, 24-month goals, and dream goals relate to each other, here are a couple of examples.

- Let's say the dream goal is to become a teacher trainer with 20 graduates per year, so a reasonable 24-month goal would be to complete the 300-hour training program, which is required in order for you to become an E-RYT 500 (an experienced, registered yoga teacher at the 500-hour level). This means that a 12-month goal would be to begin a 300-hour training program. In 24 months you might not reach your dream goal, but you will be well on your way to it and have removed the obstacles that keep you from beginning to train teachers, which is your ultimate dream goal. It is quite likely that your future development into this new yoga service will also create a needed revenue stream for you to reach your financial goals. In our current sample, you can imagine running a teacher training program in year four, which will add $35,000 to your income.
- The dream goal is to become a published author. A reasonable 24-month goal would be to draft the manuscript of the book. Your 12-month goal could be to write an outline of the book and the first chapter, as well as eliminating one of your weekly classes so that you can dedicate time to writing each week.

Real Talk

"When you have a business, you can try almost all of your ideas, and the ones that stick are the ones you water and let grow."
Cyndi Lee
Teacher of mindful yoga and author

Only you can judge how realistic your goals are, and I will be the last person to squash anyone's big dreams. Your dream goal will be achieved by accumulating revenue earned within each of your service areas year over year. This gives you an opportunity to operate realistically and to be creative while thinking about how you are going to hit those goals.

CREATE BRIDGE STRATEGIES

It's now time to create bridge strategies, which are the stepping stones that lead from where you are now to where you want to be. Your aim with this exercise is to add a bridge strategy to implement for each of your service models—although you can choose more than one. Bridge strategies are bountiful, and there are most likely a handful of creative ways that you can reach your goals in each of your service areas.

Here are tips for creating bridge strategies:

- What is the literal difference between where you are and where you want to be? For example, if you have 4 private clients and would like to have 10, the difference is 6. A bridge strategy could be to obtain 6 new private clients by starting a referral program with your existing private clients.
- Do you need help to achieve the scope of your dreams? A powerful bridge strategy for growth can be to build a team by adding members who can help you do more within your business. For instance, adding administrative support.
- Who from your hot list (see chapter 17, page 180) can help you to reach your goals? A great bridge strategy may include creating a connection with a person or company from your hot list.

- What kind of preparation, training, designation, licensing, or registration is required to accomplish your goals? For instance, if your dream is launching an e-commerce website, you'll need a business license and state sales tax ID. You will also need to build out the website itself. A 12-month goal might be to create a master task list for the e-commerce process. Your bridge strategy could be taking a small-business workshop so that you fully understand what you need to do to make your e-commerce website a reality.
- Do obstacles stand in your way of reaching your goals? For example, do you have enough resources (time or money) to obtain your E-YRT 500 in 24 months? If not, then you will need to get creative in developing a bridge strategy to work around your obstacles. Finding creative solutions for obstacles is tricky for yoga business owners because their nose is against the wall of the problem when they are the one that is dealing with it.
- If you find yourself facing an obstacle that you cannot see around, get an outside opinion from someone with an objective perspective. Share your obstacle with someone who is not involved in it and ask them to help you find a way around it. This strategy works. I believe that nearly every problem has a solution. You might be limited in your ability to see them because of your proximity to the problem, but someone from the outside looking in is quite likely to be able to help you.

To begin determining bridge strategies, I like to first refer back to the business maximization worksheet from chapter 11 (see figure 11.1 on page 115). Each of the opportunities you listed to maximize your business are bridge strategies for creating growth. Now is your chance to put them to work in your yoga business in support of your dreams. Often, taking the first step toward your dream goals is simply manipulating your existing business using a customer base you already have. It's so important to make the most of what you can right where you are now; this is why I encourage you to maximize first when considering bridge strategies.

Next, I use what I call the bridge strategy worksheet (see figure 18.3) and write into the bridge strategy column the strategies from the business maximization worksheet that I can use to help me achieve my 12- or 24-month midpoint goals. Remember, a bridge strategy may be used more than once! After you've incorporated your opportunities to maximize into your bridge strategies, now take time to consider new bridge strategies. It is very important at this phase of your business planning that every single service model has a bridge strategy.

Finally, when identifying your dream goals, be aware that some are more straightforward. For instance, dream goals of earning $25,000 in one-to-one revenue in six years or increasing your email list to 10,000, require you to simply keep building your list, keep expanding your client base and essentially keep doing more of what works. Some of your bigger dream goals such as becoming a published author or securing conference and festival appearances require a bit more creativity and work to realize. Also be aware that some of your bridge strategies will work and some will fail. This is a normal part of running your yoga business. And, as we experienced with the pandemic, on occasion there will be circumstances completely out of your control. During these times you will also have to adjust your bridge strategies.

Be bold and get creative. At the end of the day, it is going to be up to you to figure out how to reach your goals and it starts here with solid bridge strategies, midpoint goals and a dedication to doing the work.

FIGURE 18.3 Sample Bridge Strategy Worksheet

Service model	Starting revenue	12-month goal	Bridge strategy	12-month revenue	24-month goal	Bridge strategy	24-month revenue	Bridge strategy	Dream goal	By when?
One-to-one sessions	$0	Sell 40 private sessions at $125 per session	Add private sessions to website as singles and packages; offer current students free private consultation (20 min) and free session (45 min) if they refer a friend	$5,000	Sell 100 private sessions at $150 per session	Increase price of privates by $25 per session	$15,000	TBD	Earn $25,000 per year	6 years
Group sessions	$30,000	Add one additional weekly class	Request an additional class at my existing studio or interview at a new studio	$35,000	Increase revenue	Renegotiate my per class fee; increase attendance by marketing to larger email list	$40,000	TBD	Earn $50,000/ year	6 years
Conferences and festivals	$0	Build solid relationships with producers; build list of 10 local and regional conferences or festivals and the contacts for booking	Attend one conference or festival and introduce myself to the producer		Pitch myself to 10 conferences or festivals	Write a sample pitch letter and record a sample video of myself teaching		TBD	Teach at two conferences or festivals per year and earn $5,000	6 years

(continued)

FIGURE 18.3 Sample Bridge Strategy Worksheet *(continued)*

Service model	Starting revenue	12-month goal	Bridge strategy	12-month revenue	24-month goal	Bridge strategy	24-month revenue	Bridge strategy	Dream goal	By when?
Workshops	$0	Create and lead series of in-person workshops	Write a weekend workshop series and offer it for free at my home yoga studio in exchange for feedback and testimonials	$0	Sell two weekend workshops per year	Write sample pitch letter, including testimonials, and secure two weekend workshops at my home yoga studio	$5,000	TBD	Travel 4 times per year to lead workshops and earn $10,000	24 months
Immersions	$0							TBD		
Retreats	$0	Find both a regional and international location and run a sample budget for each in the tour calculator	Connect with three key contacts about their experience running retreats and ask for a recommendation of location; exchange for social media posts of their upcoming retreats	$0	Run first regional retreat with eight participants	create a 12-month marketing plan to sell retreat and implement it	$12,500	TBD	Host one retreat and have one week vacation each year and earn $12,500	24 months

Service model	Starting revenue	12-month goal	Bridge strategy	12-month revenue	24-month goal	Bridge strategy	24-month revenue	Bridge strategy	Dream goal	By when?
Trainings	*$0*	*Begin a 300-hour training program*	*Research 300-hour training programs*	*$0*	*Complete 300- hour training program*		*$0*	*Become E-RYT 500 and create my yoga school; hire an admin assistant*	*Become a teacher trainer with 20 graduates per year and earn $35,000*	*10 years*
Products and merchandise	*$0*	*Write table of contents and first chapter of my book*	*Add a writing block once a month to my schedule*	*$0*	*Complete the manuscript for my book*	*Add a writing block once a week to my schedule*	*$0*	*TBD*	*Become a published author*	*6 years*
	$0	*Complete my favorite brands list and grow my email list to 1,500*	*Add landing page with free offer to my website*	*$0*	*Grow my email list to 3,000*	*Contribute two articles with backlinks for the yoga studios I teach at to increase traffic to my website*		*TBD*	*Secure a paid ambassador relationship with one of my favorite brands; email list of 10,000*	*6 years*
Income	***$30,000***	-	-	***$40,000***	-	-	***$72,500***	-	***Earn $150,000 per year***	***10 years***

Your Yoga Business Homework

Choose Bridge Strategies

The goal of this activity is to determine how you will move from your starting point to your 12-month midpoint goal and from your 12-month midpoint goal to your 24-month goal. You will also be able to witness how your income or revenue grows as you move from one goal to the next. Use the worksheet in figure 18.4 to help you choose your bridge strategies and provide you with a complete 24-month business plan to help you achieve your dreams.

FIGURE 18.4 Bridge Strategy Worksheet

Service model	Starting revenue	12-month goal	Bridge strategy	12-month revenue	24-month goal	Bridge strategy	24-month revenue	Bridge strategy	Dream goal	By when?
One-to-one sessions										
Group sessions										
Confer-ences and festivals										
Workshops										
Immersions										
Retreats										
Trainings										
Products and mer-chandise										

From A. Taylor, *Your Yoga Business*. (Champaign, IL: Human Kinetics, 2024). Available online on HK*Propel*.

When I think back over the progress which has been made—across all of the yoga businesses that I have watched develop—there is one thing that stands out above all else: the effort required to arrive. Once the plan is complete (and yours is now complete!), you must show up daily to work your plan and continuously put in the effort toward becoming your dreams. It is this effort, this daily showing up, which ultimately determines your success and ultimately determines your journey.

PART VI
GET IT DONE

19
MASTER THE BIG FOUR

The progress of your yoga business depends on your ability to successfully execute across multiple functions of your business at the same time. Not only do you need to deliver a consistently great product, but you also need to function as a marketer, an accountant, a strategist, and an operations manager. These are the four essential areas of your business that you must work on regularly in order to move your business forward. They are so vital to your overall business that you can think of them as the wheels of a car. If one wheel is missing, the car won't get very far, and the ride will be difficult.

One of our original taglines at YAMA was "We help teachers do what they do best: Teach."

Our value proposition at that time was that we would take on the required responsibilities of marketing, finances, strategy, and operations so that our clients could focus on creating and delivering great products. At YAMA we refer to strategy, operations, marketing, and finances as the big four. For the clients whose businesses we manage, we look after the big four on their behalf. I am confident that with this book you can successfully master the big four for your business yourself!

Do you ever wonder why some of the best yoga teachers don't have more substantial businesses? There's more than one answer to this question, but one of the reasons is usually because it can range from difficult to nearly impossible for some yoga teachers to capably manage the other vital functions within their businesses. A one-wheel car simply doesn't get anywhere.

Real Talk

"Aside from being a yoga teacher, you end up having to do all the roles: cleaner, social media person, marketing person, banking person . . . and my biggest lesson was having the grace to step into all these roles and being patient to wait for the business to develop. Sometimes it takes a while for the magic beans to grow."
Finlay Wilson
Founder of Heart Space, a yoga not-for-profit, and creator of Kilted Yoga

One of my long-term clients is a yoga teacher and studio owner named Selena Isles. During our initial conversations, I asked her who was on her team. She replied, "Me; Mo who handles communication, newsletters, and any communication between hiring bodies and me; and Karen who handles administrative tasks, contracts, legal, and money." And then she started giggling hysterically. I asked her what was so funny, and she said, "Well, Mo and Karen don't really exist. I am Mo and Karen." Then I started laughing hysterically, too.

Selena knew instinctively that there were different functions of her business that needed tending to, and until she could hire a team by working with YAMA, she split herself into multiple people with distinct duties (Mo and Karen even had separate email addresses!) in order to build the team she knew her business needed. I love this story because it highlights how important the different roles are within your business and how they each deserve their own space and maybe even an alias!

Running a successful yoga business requires you to master the ability to switch gears and jump from function to function. This means that life as a yoga business owner is never boring, is sometimes daunting, and requires a set schedule in order to achieve results. Being responsible for performing multiple functions means that most likely you will have to do things you may not love (you can grow to love them!) or do things you are not good at for the overall success of your business. If you focus only on the "fun stuff" and ignore the rest, you will find your progress is hindered. You don't need to be an expert at every function to serve your business well, and it is important to allow yourself time to get good at things you are not good at now—the same approach that applies to your yoga teaching. You are your own small business; own it!

You are your own small business—own it!

The big four yoga business functions are strategy, operations, marketing, and finances. Let's take a deeper look at each.

STRATEGY

Strategy is the overall plan and direction of your business. Many of us are so busy running the businesses day to day that we rarely carve out time to think about where the business is going and why, what we want to build and create, and most importantly—what's working and what's not working in the business so we can pivot and adjust more quickly. Consistent time spent on strategy is important to staying efficient and to running a flexible and resilient business. The following are the components of strategy.

Goals

As we covered in chapter 11, clarifying exactly what you want to create within your business is vital to staying on track and getting it done. I like to set goals in two-year increments and refine them every year through an assessment in December as I begin to turn from year one to year two. The strategy of setting goals also includes setting financial goals for how much income you want to generate and from which of your service models this revenue will come.

Assessment

Assessment is a regular inquiry into what's working and not working in your business. As we covered in chapter 10, keeping a close eye on how your business is doing is crucial to its success. Spending time weekly asking yourself about the interactions that take place within your business will help you keep tabs on what is moving you toward success and what might be holding you back. You don't necessarily need to make changes every week based on your observations, but you do want to constantly assess your business so that nothing problematic or opportune goes unnoticed. In this way, you can see when the time is right to make a small shift here or a small shift there to get the results that will move you toward your goals. As we covered in depth in chapter 10, regularly considering the numerous small shifts you can make across your business can have a major impact. This is called maximization.

Research

Research is gathering the information needed in order to understand opportunities, make decisions, and set goals. Spending time gathering this information is important when we want to do something we know nothing about. Whether it's developing a new service model or using a new communication channel, we often don't know what it will entail. You wouldn't want to marry someone that you've never gone out with before. But that's exactly what we do over and over again within our yoga businesses.

Research time is time to think creatively, brainstorm, and generate ideas about what's next. I give myself regular time each week to dream. I love to do this on Sunday mornings with my coffee in bed—great dreams breed great goals. Whether it's time spent researching on the Internet, reading books and magazines, or hopping on the phone with someone you respect to chat through an idea or explore a potential new business opportunity, giving yourself time and space to think and dream is important.

Research also includes time spent learning and studying the new tools you want to use in your business, such as mastering how your website or email marketing software functions. People are often paralyzed by the things they don't know how to do, but the truth is, they also don't spend time learning and studying how to use the tools to begin with. And oftentimes it's a lot easier than they think.

I also consider time spent networking as research time because these are important hours that you spend out in the community connecting with people and uncovering new relationships and opportunities. It's a bit of in-person research, if you will.

Event Planning

The administrative, logistical, and sales and marketing tasks required to lead events take a lot of time to complete. Often when yoga professionals plan out the year and put events on the calendar (or price their events), they underestimate this time. This is why it's important to carve out consistent time every week to work toward bringing your events to fruition. Chapter 6 is where you can find the tasks related to event planning.

Product Concept Planning

As we have covered in chapter 8, Menu of Services, developing and revising the pricing, packaging, and prioritizing of your goods and services are crucial to your business working well. Creating a strong menu of services must be done, and it also must be revised regularly. Many folks decide what they want to sell, then build it, sell it, and let it stagnate. All too often I work with yoga professionals who haven't updated their pricing or packaging or shifted the priority of the products that they are selling for years. Keeping this revision strategy in mind consistently will keep your products current and timely.

Sales and Marketing Planning

Before you can work on a plan to sell and market your events and products, you have to create a sales and marketing plan. The tasks related to creating your sales and marketing plan are included in chapter 16, Create Your Marketing Schedule, and chapter 18, Identify Strategies. You will need to reserve time to build your plan.

OPERATIONS

Operations are the essential functions used to run your business. Technically speaking, the rest of the big four—strategy, marketing, and finance—are also part of your operations, but for our purposes, operations refers to the people, processes, tools, and essential infrastructure required for you to be in business. People are those on whom your business depends. Processes are the series of actions taken within your business. Tools are the instruments used to perform functions within your business, and essential infrastructure refers to the nonnegotiable items required for you to be in business. Let's take a look at the most important items related to operations for yoga business owners.

People

Just as in Selena's example earlier in the chapter, you need to spend time thinking about who is helping you become your dream. Getting help is crucial to your success as a yoga business owner, whether this means cultivating relationships with a mentor, an assistant, a coach, a group of peers, an intern, or a client. Cultivating the relationship includes initiating the relationship, clarifying the expectations, and then, of course, spending time with the people on whom your business depends.

Processes

As a small-business owner, you are the business's most important resource. This is especially true when your business is yoga because you not only have to organize and run the business, but you also have to teach and deliver the product. Building and refining your time management process is vital to running your business. We will cover best practices for time management in chapter 20, Act Like a Boss.

Savvy yoga business owners Young Ho Kim (left) and Matt Giordano (center) know that time spent on research is vital. Here we are learning together at the Swiss Yoga Conference.

Data management is another important process for your business. This refers to how and where you file and store your business materials. Although this may not seem important, it must not be taken lightly. Having a good storage system for filing all of the data and materials that comprise your business improves your efficiency. I keep my files organized by client management, content, data management, strategy, marketing, operations, and financials—each with subfiles organized by each year that my business is in operation. The organizing system that we discussed for your marketing materials in chapter 16 is an example of a data management system being put to work. When you can easily find things that you need and when you can easily access the historical database of what your business has done, it provides a clean foundation from which to grow. I had a fabulous intern once, Lisa, whose entire role was to help organize the back office after I had been in business for eight years. The data management system she put in place is priceless to me to this day.

Managing your contact lists, such as your hot 20 and favorite brands, also falls under data management. Your lists need to be tidied and updated regularly. In fact, I always have my eyes peeled for new contacts and potential business partners. When something or someone becomes apparent as a possible new partner, I add that contact to my list for distribution later.

Tools

Tools include the software and subscriptions you need to run your business. Tools also include your phone, Internet provider, email marketing and bookkeeping software, and extra storage needed for your data such as Dropbox. Your website host, video host, and e-commerce solution for collecting payments on your website are also tools.

Essential Infrastructure

When building a yoga business, there is a myriad of structures that you could choose to use to operate. Here are those that I find to be essential and those that truly matter to your business.

Insurance

Insurance for yoga teachers is essential for every business that teaches yoga to clients. Search online for liability insurance for yoga teachers to find options for kinds of insurance and providers. Cross reference your selection with other teachers in the community before signing up!

Licenses and Certifications

The licenses and certifications you need to run your business depend on what kind of yoga professional you are. Be sure the certification and license from the granting organization—for example, International Association of Yoga Therapists, Yoga Alliance, or accreditation from the yoga school you graduated from—are up to date so you can maintain an active status and continue to deliver your services.

Legal Structure

Legal structure refers to the tax ID number and the selection and formation of a business entity such as a limited liability company (LLC). I recommend forming an LLC and having a separate bank account and tax ID number for your business. While you are just getting started, it may not seem necessary to separate yourself from your business, as you literally are the business. However, the bigger and more successful your business becomes, the more clearly you will want to differentiate your business from your individual self, and forming a separate company is how this is done.

MARKETING

In part IV, we discussed the plethora of marketing channels, techniques, and strategies you can use to communicate about your business and the goods and services you sell. Once you have decided on the channels, techniques, and strategies you will use, you need to develop a weekly workflow. I organize my marketing into the following groups: planning, production, and distribution. Planning refers to the creation of your marketing plan, production refers to the content that needs to be created in order to execute your plan, and distribution refers to sharing the content across your marketing channels. The following are the most important marketing tasks for yoga business owners.

- *Planning*: As covered in chapter 16, organize your marketing schedule in three-month increments leading up to your events. This means entering the date for the event or launch and working backward to add the necessary tasks. Also refer to the section Sales and Marketing Planning on page 198 in this chapter.
- *Production*: Before you can distribute content, you need to produce it, so it's important to carve out time every week to produce content, otherwise you won't be able to keep up with your distribution schedule. Production includes writing copy for email marketing, blogs, and social media posts. It also includes writing copy for pitches you will present to create new opportunities for yourself. Production also includes designing hard copy marketing materials, taking pictures, and recording and editing videos.
- *Distribution*: Distribution refers to the time needed to share content across your communication channels. This includes time spent posting on social media; scheduling email marketing; updating your website with new events, goods, and services; dropping off hard copy marketing materials at physical locations, and pitching for new opportunities. No matter what form it takes, you need to consistently reserve time weekly to distribute your marketing content.

FINANCES

It's important to understand clearly how your business is doing financially and to keep on top of your business's finances. I like to think of these two tasks as analysis and upkeep. These tasks help you understand how your money works in your business, manage your incoming monies and outgoing expenses, and keep an eye on how your pricing relates to it all.

Monthly, quarterly, and annual cash flow analyses provide a regular look at how your money moves in your business. I look at mine every week now. When I first began analyzing my finances, I disliked the task, but now I find it empowering and reassuring, especially after making mistakes and learning the hard way what the business could afford. If I had been looking at my finances more closely and regularly, I could have stopped overspending sooner. I urge you to analyze your cash monthly, quarterly, and annually and to put dates on your calendar to review your cash flow.

Upkeep is vital because good financial health, as with much of what we have discussed in *Your Yoga Business*, isn't the result of magic, but rather consistency. Therefore, tasks that may seem inconsequential, such as bookkeeping and paying bills and taxes, are actually terribly important. Trust me, you do not want revenue agents to come looking for you. Yoga professionals used to be able to fly under the radar with regard to taxes, but this is not the case any longer. And, if the tax agent does come knocking, you want your financial files to be tidy and up to date to prevent your business from coming to a standstill while you try to produce the requested paperwork. It has happened. Set time aside every week to do your bookkeeping and to pay your bills. It is so much easier to do this in small, consistent chunks of time rather than waiting until the end of the year and doing it all at once.

The other important component of upkeep is to be consistent about collecting the payments that are owed to you by preparing and sending invoices and sending collection request communications to people who are late with payments. Seeing to these vital tasks each week keeps the cash flowing into your business.

MASTERING THE BIG FOUR

Knowing what the big four are and mastering them are two different things, and I believe that mastering the big four is one of the most important things you can do as a small-business owner, and maybe the single most important. Remember the analogy of the car missing a wheel? Well, if you want to go the distance with your business, all four wheels (the big four) need to be on the car and in good shape. Even if you are making progress in your yoga business without properly focusing on all four areas, eventually it will catch up with you. Overcompensating in one of the big four does not eliminate the necessity of the others. For instance, you can be the world's best marketer, but at some point, you will have to itemize your expenses, file your taxes, and set goals.

Here are two tried-and-tested strategies for mastering the big four as a busy entrepreneur. First, create a task block that occurs once a week for each of the big four by subtask (take a look at figure 19.1 for an example of how I might include task blocks for the big four in my workweek). You can do anything for an hour and a half, and you must. Sometimes I set a timer and race myself to the end of the 90-minute task block. It's important that when the time you have allotted for the task expires, you move on to the next task. It is much better to make small and consistent progress in all of the big four than to make progress in only one. You may find that some functions require more than one task block each week in order to keep up with the workload. For instance, I have two weekly task blocks for finances: one for analysis and one for upkeep. There is nothing sillier than having a stack of invoices that need to be generated sitting on your desk for longer than a week! Figure out the time you need to make sure you can send those invoices.

Second, seek help if you need it. Don't avoid a task like bookkeeping or recording and editing videos because you don't know how to accomplish it. There are ways to get help for all yoga businesses and within all budgets. If you cannot afford to hire someone to do the task for you, you might be able to pay them to teach you what you need to know so that you can do the work yourself. We've already discussed ways to get affordable help, so do not let your lack of certain skills keep you from completing important tasks within your business.

FIGURE 19.1 Sample Weekly Workflow with Task Blocks for the Big Four

	Monday	Tuesday	Wednesday	Thursday	Friday	Saturday	Sunday
8:00 am	Morning routine						
9:00 am		Commute	Email				
10:00 am	Group (90 min)	One-to-one (60 min)		Group (90 min)	Group (90 min)	Yoga	Cook-ing and meal prep
11:00 am		Commute					
12:00 pm	Lunch						
1:00 pm		One-to-one (60 min)					
2:00 pm							Family
3:00 pm	**ADMIN (STRATEGY + OPERATIONS)**	Commute		**ADMIN (MARKETING)**	**ADMIN (FINANCIALS)**		
4:00 pm		One-to-one (60 min)				One-to-one (60 min)	
5:00 pm							
6:00 pm		Gym			Gym	Errands and shopping	
7:00 pm	Dinner						
8:00 pm							
9:00 pm	Admin and create content			Admin and Netflix	Time with friends		
10:00 pm							
11:00 pm							
12:00 pm							

Real Talk

"You can have a great idea, but if you can't manifest it, then who cares?"
Cyndi Lee
Teacher of mindful yoga and author

Note that time spent communicating via email and reaching for inbox zero every day is not considered part of the big four. While email is a necessary part of your day-to-day communication, it is not an essential part of what it will take to move your business forward. Have you ever spent the whole day emailing but did not seem to get anything done? Don't fool yourself into believing that time spent emailing is important administrative time.

Your Yoga Business Homework
Revamp Your Workweek

In chapter 10 you assessed how you spend your time as a business owner. You were assigned a task to analyze your weekly workflow for seven days to look for changes you could make immediately that would give you more time for working on your business.

In this activity, you will download the blank weekly workflow template from HK*Propel* (instructions are provided at the front of this book) and build on the concept of your ideal workweek by adding a task block to your schedule for each of the big four—strategy, operations, marketing, and financials (see my example in figure 19.1 for guidance). Each task block should last 60 to 90 minutes.

Available online on HK*Propel*.

Running a successful yoga business requires a lot more skill than simply being a great yoga teacher. Understanding this and creating time management practices that ensure you can work on all of the elements required to move your business forward will go a long way to helping you reach the finish line. I have seen many incredible yoga teachers also become incredible marketers, accountants, strategists, and operations managers.

20
ACT LIKE A BOSS

You are your own small business, and whether you like it or not, you are responsible for and in charge of this entire yoga business—which makes you *the boss*. Based on my experience, there are a few important skills most yoga teachers need to cultivate in order to step fully into the role of being the boss: time management, learning to make clear agreements, and the art of negotiation. We will discuss them all in this chapter.

MANAGE YOUR TIME

I have an amazing photo of Sadie Nardini (before her mohawk, but still 100 percent rock 'n' roll) in the kitchen of her apartment in Brooklyn holding up a piece of white paper, drawn all over with a black marker. She has an enormous smile. What was drawn on the paper was nothing more than an outline of a well-scheduled day. As a budding entrepreneur, she was trying to figure out how on earth to get everything done that needed to be done in order to build the business of her dreams, and the simple task we completed together of properly organizing her time was monumental.

Being successful is sexy, but oftentimes what is required to become successful is not. Contrary to what most people want to believe about the creative process, it's less magic wand and more pulling weeds. It's really about getting a little bit done every single day that makes your dreams come true. Being successful means sitting down to a work session when you aren't in the mood or flipping your smartphone upside down to minimize distractions. It means getting on your mat on those off days, where a full practice might end up being nothing more than a long savasana, or it means keeping your goals literally visible—on a sticky note right in front of your face. As the familiar Instagram meme goes, "Beyoncé wasn't built in a day." This means that important work takes time, and the important work of fulfilling your big dreams takes well-managed time, which is why great time management is crucial.

I'll never forget that day at Sadie's. She was mind blown after creating that structure for herself and seeing that the power to achieve her dreams was in her own hands. Fast-forward 10 years, and Sadie has groomed herself into one of the most productive entrepreneurs I know, having mastered the balance of daily work and daily reward that works best for her. This allows her to maintain one of the most elusive of business skills: consistency.

I cannot express enough how important cultivating good time management is for an entrepreneur. Big goals and big dreams are nothing more than the accumulation of small daily wins. Unless you have major investment money and can hire a huge team to help you do it all at once, it's going to be up to you to move your business forward each day.

Big goals and big dreams are nothing more than the accumulation of small daily wins.

One of my greatest inspirations for time management and maintaining entrepreneurial creativity is a book called *The Creative Habit: Learn It and Use It for Life* by Twyla Tharp, a prolific artist, creator, and choreographer. In it, Tharp says,

> Creativity is no mystery; it is the product of hard work and preparation, of knowing one's aims and one's subject, of learning from approaches taken in the past. It's a process undertaken every day. It's a habit. Creativity is a habit and the best creativity is the result of good work habits. That's it in a nutshell.

A habit is nothing more than a regular practice—like your yoga practice. In our day-to-day lives we all have good habits, bad habits, habits we want more of, and habits we need to let go of. Creating good work habits is critical to your achieving your big dreams. I'm excited to share with you the time management best practices that I've developed through the years as technology, priorities, family, and requirements of the industry have changed.

Nurturing your yoga business is a marathon, which means that not every leg of the race will be an all-out sprint. At times you will rest, recuperate, and refuel. At times you will stay up all night to meet deadlines. The full distance in the marathon is covered by keeping pace, and this is accomplished through good time management. Time management can be intimidating, overwhelming, and even elusive—a day can slip through your fingers. And your external constraints and obligations can be frustrating and limiting, but with good work habits you can win (most of) your days and, most importantly, make real progress toward becoming your dreams.

So let's look at time management best practices.

Keep a to-do list.

When I start working for the day, I take a look at the day's scheduled appointments and task blocks. I consider what isn't finished from the previous workday and review what tasks might be urgent for the current day. Based on those observations, I create a priority list of what is important and nonnegotiable to complete for the day. For everything else there is to do, there will be tomorrow or the next scheduled task block. It is important to remember that you cannot do it all and that you cannot do everything *now*. Working toward long-term goals may not seem like a priority when assessing what to accomplish in a day, but it is important not to miss taking those small steps of progress. At the end of the day, cross off what was completed and prepare to make a new list.

Create a priority list of what is important and nonnegotiable to complete for the day.

Prioritize.

It is up to you to make sure that you focus on what matters each day. Use your big four task blocks and other tools to keep your attention where it needs to be.

Minimize distractions.

Smartphones, direct messaging, email notifications, and the Internet are all tools that provide the amazing access and flexibility that allow us to thrive as yoga entrepreneurs. These are also the very same tools that create a gauntlet of distractions at every turn. Distractions are real and can erode your daily progress, ability to focus, and bottom line. When I sit down for a task block with a to-do list, I put my smartphone out of reach. The work-from-home office environment—which for many includes children learning online, partners also working from home, and everyone spending a lot of time in the house together—provides its own unique set of realities. Yet, even in work-from-home environments, we must do our best to manage distractions.

Focus on one task and track your time.

I am a strong believer in doing one task at a time in 90-minute increments. Set a timer and get to work! When the clock is ticking, it's like being on your very own productivity game show. You're in charge of moving on to the next task, and working for a set amount of time can make getting work done more tolerable and even fun!

Start now.

You already know that "Beyoncé wasn't built in a day" and that it will take time to become your dreams, so what are you waiting for? There will never going to be a perfect time or perfect work conditions in which to begin—so stop procrastinating.

Set up a good (beautiful) work space.

A beautiful, functional work space affects your overall well-being, creativity, and productivity. Think about ways that you can beautify your work space. Essentials include an ergonomic desk and chair combination, sufficient lighting, limited clutter, and inspiring eye candy, such as a family photo or fresh flowers.

Make your workday a ritual.

By making the start of your workday part of a familiar sequence, you replace doubt and fear with comfort and routine. It's like stepping onto a well-worn yoga mat. Whether that ritual is lighting a candle, grabbing your favorite coffee cup, playing music that helps you focus, or flipping over your smartphone, building routine into your workday allows for maximum productivity. I usually light a candle; turn on soothing lo-fi music; and have coffee, water, and a snack close at hand.

Take breaks.

This one is contrary to what we think is required in order to get stuff done. Is anyone else out there guilty of skipping meals or sitting in one place for an extraordinarily long time? Getting up from your desk, stretching, taking a walk, or eating might seem like it is keeping you from making progress, but it is actually doing the opposite. These breaks give you a chance to refocus, reset, and refuel, making you more effective in the long run. The pandemic gave us a great opportunity to reimagine the workday, how we take our breaks, and how we spend our time. I will not skip lunch ever again, and as long as I am working from home, there will be nap breaks scheduled as a nonnegotiable part of my day.

Schedule tasks well.

As entrepreneurs, our greatest luxury is our ability to schedule our own time, and yet quite often we don't set a schedule that works for us. When scheduling, ask yourself these questions: Does this schedule work for me? Do I have time to rest, refuel, and go to the bathroom between appointments? Do I have a cushion of time for travel delays? Am I taking this appointment at a time that works for my client, but not for me? Have I made time for what is important for *me* each day? Have I allowed time to address the big four, my personal practice, or dinner with my family? Are there gaps or fragments in my day that add up to an unusable loss of time?

Reward yourself.

I mentioned earlier how Sadie came up with the perfect balance of daily work and daily reward for herself. Everyone's rewards are different, and for Sadie, this means completing her priority to-do list, then having a small glass of white wine and daydreaming into her journal. What can you give to yourself each day as a small pat on the back for making progress toward your goals? Is it 15 minutes scrolling on Instagram? (But be sure to set a timer so you don't get sucked in for hours!) Is it a quick text exchange with a loved one, a nap? A silver lining of good time management is that the better your work habits are, the better your nonwork possibilities can be. While living in Germany's highly productive society for four years, I witnessed first-hand how working efficiently each day means longer lunches, going home earlier, more bank holidays, more vacations, and taking less stress home from the office.

CRAFT CLEAR AGREEMENTS

We have a saying around the office: Clarity is queen. As someone who negotiates contracts day in and day out, the importance of clarity when making an agreement is obvious. In my role as a business manager, I am regularly in the middle of an opportunity between two parties who would like to cooperate or collaborate in some way.

Within the agreement, each party gives something and each party gets something. For me to agree to an opportunity on behalf of my client, I must clearly understand exactly what the give is and what the get is. A collaboration to me is something tactile or physical; it is a stack of paperwork that is black and white in my hands and on my desk. It's something that is tangible and can be edited, corrected, and negotiated. It's something that can be referred to when we need to check in and make sure that what we are delivering (giving) and what we are receiving (getting) are correct according to the agreement. It makes it so much easier when things get off track if we have a clear agreement in the middle.

Owning your own small business means you have to learn to Act Like a Boss.

The clearer we are at the beginning of the collaboration and during the making of the agreement, the easier it is to execute the collaboration and the easier it is to argue the agreement if problems arise. And trust me, problems arise. YAMA was one of the first companies to advocate for the wide use of contracts in the yoga industry to clarify the terms of the business arrangement between parties working together. While not every situation calls for a fully signed agreement, every collaboration with another party needs a detailed and agreed-on set of working terms and expectations that clearly state the terms of the arrangement.

Real Talk

"Don't be too strict. Create rules, but be flexible."
Dharma Mittra
Yoga teacher, practitioner, and guru of modern yoga

The yoga space—although it is maturing—is still predominantly a mom-and-pop space, where many of us are doing business with friends, significant others, colleagues, cousins, friends of boyfriends, friends of colleagues, friends of cousins, our teachers, our students, and so on. All of this breeds enormous amounts of creativity and opportunity. I mean, how amazing is it that pretty much everyone you know is a potential business partner? However, the familial nature of our industry also breeds opportunities for things to go wrong because it's hard to get specific and to talk in business terms with the people you know, love, and trust.

Most mistakes and things that go wrong in a collaboration are not caused by malicious intent. The things that go wrong do so because people didn't anticipate or plan for them. The cause usually is not because one party tries intentionally to get one over on or take advantage of the other party. As entrepreneurs in a maturing market, we are trying new things or doing new things together for the first time. We are all riding the learning curve together. So the clearer we can be in the planning stages—anticipating and clarifying both positive and negative outcomes of the collaboration—the better off our collaboration will be.

I could write an entire book on what I have learned (the hard way!) while creating and participating in thousands of collaborations across the globe, but I've distilled it to the nitty-gritty for you here. So, what needs to be clarified within a collaboration? Let's take a look!

The give.

Start with a detailed scope of work (task overview). You can only own what you understand, and you want an extremely high level of understanding of every collaboration. What exactly is the opportunity you are being presented with? Ask questions to gather information until you can unambiguously describe what you are expected to do.

The get.

Now that your task is clear, it is time to consider what you are receiving for completing the task. Is the monetary or nonmonetary compensation adequate when weighed against the task? Are resources needed to complete the task? If so, are those costs included in the compensation or considerations? For example, is travel or lodging required or the creation of and transfer of content such as large video files. What are the payment terms? Are you required to pay up front for expenses or to put in a considerable amount of time on behalf of the project before receiving compensation? These are all important questions to clarify.

The full scope.

When making a clear agreement you need to understand what you are responsible for and what your partner is responsible for. I call this the *full scope of work*. As your collaboration develops, be clear in outlining what each party needs to do in order to deliver the agreed-on goal.

The deadline.

Someday is on no one's calendar. A due date is required to drive attention and drive action. Be realistic rather than optimistic in your time estimates, and agree on a deadline that you can successfully meet. If the task is large, break it into steps, each with its own deadline. I almost always ask for more time than I think I need when determining the full scope of work. Especially today, while we're still experiencing repercussions of the pandemic, timelines seem to rarely work out how you think they will.

The divorce.

You already know what the give and get are, but what happens or what is the consequence if you or the other party doesn't successfully complete the task? Usually, two parties decide to collaborate when they are in love, so you need to consider your opportunity past the honeymoon stage. What if the other party in the relationship isn't who you thought you "were marrying or getting in bed with"? What if you fall in love with or want to collaborate with someone else; are you free to do so? If exclusivity is part of the agreement, then other collaborations may be out of the question. Although this marriage analogy is a bit tongue in cheek, let's take it a step further and consider divorce. This scenario is rarely considered, especially when doing business with people you know, love, and trust. Ironically, considering the possibility of divorce is actually a relationship preserver because when both parties think through the divorce scenario together up front, there will be fewer surprises in the long run.

Keep these essential components of how to craft a clear agreement close at hand as you create new opportunities for your business—even if the collaborations are casual in nature—and continue to work on developing the keen eye and skills you need to make clear agreements. It is vital to your business.

Real Talk

"I am a man of my word. If someone makes an order, I try to deliver the product. If someone pays for class, I try to be there. It's called being responsible and being honest . . . I just don't think there's anything more important than integrity and responsibility. If you want to be successful, you gotta deliver what you say you're gonna deliver. You better have something that works."

Bryan Kest

Yoga practitioner, teacher, and creator of Power Yoga

LEARN THE ART OF NEGOTIATION

The last bit of your transition into being a boss is to learn the art of negotiation. Since starting my business in 2010, I have been part of thousands of exchanges between my clients and the media outlets, brands, and venues that they have worked with. Becoming an expert negotiator requires experience; there's really no way around it. You have to go through round after round of negotiations with client after client and partner after partner in order to begin to see the similarities in each exchange, the likelihood of outcomes, and the patterns in behavior for both you and your partner. It will come with time.

Luckily, I am sharing the best of what I have learned with you here to help you start acting like a boss as soon as possible. They don't call me the Ari Gold of yoga for nothing.

Opportunity Cost

In economics, *opportunity cost* is defined as the loss of potential gain from other alternatives when one alternative is chosen. More easily said, opportunity cost is the value of what cannot be had from one activity when you say yes to another activity. For instance, in that single session that we've based so much of our pricing rationale on, you can only do one thing at a time. As Granny used to say, "You can't dance at two parties at once."

So when you say yes to teaching a one-to-one session for a client, then you must say no to doing any other thing in your life during that hour. Here's an example: If you are offered the opportunity to teach a workshop on Friday from 10 a.m. to 1 p.m. at a rate of $300, when considering whether or not to say yes or whether or not to negotiate for more money, you need to consider the class you will miss on Friday morning that pays $80. When you calculate your opportunity cost, the workshop is actually paying you $220. This number is the one from which you should negotiate.

Depending on when this hour is within your day or on your calendar, you may say no to something more valuable and important. Consider this: If an opportunity to teach out of town arises on a weekend that you have a family engagement scheduled, then the opportunity cost of saying yes is very high, possibly even "priceless," like those old MasterCard commercials used to say. But a good negotiator will try to put a price tag on it, a high one. Someone would have to pay a heck of a premium to get me to miss my best friend's 50th birthday for instance—but for enough money, I just might consider it.

Not all opportunity costs are so extreme when you say yes, but there is always an opportunity cost for each activity that you decide to participate in. The reason this concept is so important when negotiating is because you must consider not only the give and get of the opportunity itself but also what is lost to you when you say yes. As we discussed in chapter 5, the value of your time changes as your business and reputation grow, which means that your opportunity costs will also change. Once you have an abundance of opportunities (it will happen!), you will find that you are no longer able to say yes to opportunities that used to be exciting and desirable—unless, of course, they pay you the same amount of money as your new opportunities. And it never hurts to ask for that.

Understanding a Fair Deal

A fair deal is a deal in which both parties feel adequately compensated in exchange for receiving something of equal value. This is where the give and get are considered fair by both parties involved. You need to weigh the scales until you can both get it right.

After all, an offer is just the "hello." When someone initially approaches you about an opportunity, you often think that their initial offer is the only offer because that is all they've put forth. A good negotiator knows that an initial offer is just a starting point—the beginning of a conversation—and that there are many levers, both monetary and nonmonetary, that can be pulled in order to come up with the offer that works best for both parties. It often takes multiple rounds of communication in order to arrive at the fair deal.

Going back to a client or partner who has made an initial offer is called a *counteroffer*. I have a rule of thumb to never take the first offer. This doesn't always mean that the initial offer dramatically changes before we arrive at the fair deal (e.g., they offered $500, and I was successful in obtaining $5,000). Never taking the first offer means that you are engaging your partner in a conversation about the opportunity, asking tough and thorough questions in order to clarify the give and get, and, based on the opportunity cost, making sure the rate you have been offered is appropriate. It also helps both parties find other ways to sweeten the deal.

Another reason I never take the first offer is because I am looking for ways to maximize the opportunity for everyone involved. I make a point to think creatively about what else we can bring to the partnership to add value and create a win–win. For instance, if someone wants to book a yoga teacher to model for a water company for the day, I will also make sure the partner knows that the teacher has a physical yoga studio where we could give away samples of the product.

Counteroffering is not intuitive—especially if you are negotiating for yourself—but it is a muscle that can be developed and will allow you to extract more from each opportunity or interaction. Counteroffering can also be a little bit nerve racking. It's so human to think that if you go back with a list of questions and demands (it's all in the language) that you might turn someone off from working with you and that they might pull the opportunity completely.

I'll never forget the first piece of business I did at YAMA with The Gap. I had received two phone calls on the same afternoon: one from a yoga teacher in Los Angeles and one from a yoga teacher in New York. Both were asking me to help them settle on a day rate to teach for The Gap. As fate would have it, both of these women had been offered the same opportunity, and although they didn't know each other, both of them knew to call me for guidance. I couldn't believe it!

I asked them each what day rate they were planning to request; one came back with $250, and one came back with $1,000. I thought to myself, this is incredible, and I have a moment to make a move as a negotiator. So, I asked if they would let me represent them both and take over the conversation with The Gap on their behalves. I had a strong feeling that both of their rates were off, and that if The Gap knew that they both were represented by the same agency, they would have a better shot together of getting what they were due. They both said yes, and on a Friday afternoon I took over the negotiations and made a counteroffer of $2,500 each. This was the first major opportunity that either of these teachers had received, so nerves were high! I received multiple calls from both women over the weekend. They were worried we had overbid.

Monday and Tuesday came and went with no response from The Gap. The clients were sure we'd blown the whole thing. Externally, I was patient and calm, while internally, I was a wreck, thinking perhaps I had indeed lost my first deal. On Wednesday morning I put in a call to The Gap and was greeted warmly by my contact there who blurted out, "Oh, thank god, you called. Our server went down on Friday, and none of us have had access to our emails or contacts for days. How are you? What's the rate for the clients? Okay—let's do this." Their lack of communication had nothing to do with us and nothing to do with the rates we'd given. I decided at that moment to not make up stories and to try my very best to stay patient while negotiating. You truly never know what's going on at the other person's office.

Who Sets the Pay Rate?

When asked to provide a pay rate for an opportunity, try not to be the first one to give a rate. You limit your chances of being paid a premium if you do. That being said, you have worked on understanding the value of your time and your opportunity cost, so you should be able to come up with a fair rate for yourself.

It is also important to remember that there are companies that have room within their budget to pay a premium for your services if you ask for it. If you think you might be negotiating with a company that can afford a premium rate, perhaps lead the conversation by asking, "Do you have an ideal budget in mind for the activation?" This will prompt them to give you the rate first, and what they will tell you is often much higher than what you'd have charged. Sometimes you'll go first and give a rate to which they will respond by coming back with a number that is lower based on their budget.

Here are other things to remember when negotiating:

You can't win them all.

You are not supposed to get everything you want in a negotiation; a negotiation is a give and a get, with the goal being to reach a fair deal for both parties.

Learn to say *no*.

Sometimes a fair deal is not reached, and you will say no to an opportunity. The further along you are in your career, the more you will realize that saying no is par for the course. The more opportunities you receive, the more you will realize it's simply not possible to say yes to them all and that saying no is one of the best strategies you have to help you reach your goals. You have to keep space both literally and figuratively for the things you truly want.

Don't take the negotiation personally.

A negotiation has nothing to do with you as a person. It is just business. Your partner has their priorities and you have yours. Do your best to stay neutral while negotiating.

Try to enjoy it.

Over the years, I have learned to love negotiating. I find it a very creative process to lean into what can be created within a partnership. Oftentimes, where we end up after a few rounds of negotiating is much more financially and energetically fulfilling than where the initial partnership and its offer began. Even in the rare events where nothing substantial changes there is a comfort and sense of fulfillment in knowing that a question was asked.

These days, I see pretty much every exchange I have in life as a negotiation. Whether it is a business exchange with a company or a casual social interaction with another human being, I find myself processing it all through the lens of negotiation. The lens of negotiation shapes how I perceive the wants, needs, motivations, and expectations of everyone involved (including myself). It also allows for a deeper appreciation of the complexity of each of our interactions. My practice of negotiating keeps me calm in situations where I see others get flustered and it also allows me to be satisfied when things don't go my way. Of all the many gifts and experiences that the yoga business has given me, learning to act like a boss and to be great at time management, making clear agreements, and negotiating are certainly the most consistently useful and important.

EPILOGUE

As the sun sets on another full day of writing, my thoughts turn to what the yoga business has meant to me for all these years. The yoga business has given me purpose and has been my North Star, leading me to friendships and life partners and on some of the greatest adventures around the world that I could ever have imagined.

The yoga business has motivated me every single day to wake and give my best, to wake and give my all. It has given me the freedom to pursue my dreams and to push my own limits of creativity and excellence—the heights of which only I know I am capable of. The yoga business has provided me with the most exciting and exhilarating highs and the most humbling and gut-wrenching of lows—a true spectrum of experience. The yoga business formed my professional character and gave me knowledge as a business owner that has allowed me to develop a set of skills that is transferable now into every industry: priceless know-how that no business degree could provide. The yoga business has allowed me to contribute to the world.

When I think about what the yoga business means to the clients that I have nurtured and worked with over the years, there is one phrase that comes clearly to mind: *I believe*. I believe that everything is possible, and I believe that we can become our dreams because I have seen it and witnessed it firsthand. I have witnessed how a crazy idea can turn into a real business, a real livelihood, a real life. I believe that a yoga professional with passion and commitment can become the next household name if that is what they dream of being. I believe that achieving a simple dream will allow the next dream to come. You don't need to see it all to begin. If you act on what you can see, the next step on your path forward will appear.

I believe that following your purpose allows you to find yourself over and over again, in the right place at the right time. I believe in your unique potential and in your ability to become your own wild version of success. I believe just as I did the day I decided to start YAMA that there needs to be more yoga in the world and that a key to its growth is creating thriving, sustainable yoga businesses.

It's incredibly inspiring to think back to those early days and how far we've come as an industry, what we've accomplished and developed. I am especially excited thinking about those of you who are reading this book and the dreams that you will reach and how much farther we can all go as we bring more yoga to the world. My goal with this book is to leave a legacy not only of the work that I've done and the impact that it has made but also to help create a set of tools within the space that will allow us to continue to progress as an industry.

As with all journeys, your greatest learnings and most powerful awakenings do not happen in smooth waters. They happen in times of trial and error, of innovation and iteration, and I hope that this book has done a good job of keeping it real and talking about the things that worked and the things that didn't, allowing you to learn from the rough waters in which I have sailed. I hope you found within these pages a useful gem of knowledge, a tip that will guide you through a business interaction, a conceptual understanding that raises your level of entrepreneurship and allows you to fast track your progress, and the motivation to keep going.

I wish you all from the bottom of my heart a great ride, and a successful one, that helps you reach your financial goals and allows you to grow from the beauty, joy, and sorrow of being an entrepreneur. I love yoga, and I love business. It's a thrill to me to have been able to find a way to make a living surrounded by people whom I respect and admire and to be part of a lifestyle that encourages me to live better each and every day. May you dream the impossible, and may these tools help guide you as you build your way there.

APPENDIX

Your Yoga Business Road Map

1. IDENTIFY YOUR PURPOSE

From the "Identify Your Purpose" activity in chapter 1, write your purpose statement here: ______________________________

____

2. ENVISION YOUR GREAT DREAM

Using the thoughts you gathered "Envision Your Great Dream" activity in chapter 1, write your great dream for your yoga business here:

____

____

____

____

____

____

3. REQUEST TESTIMONIALS AND FEEDBACK

Using information you gathered from the "Request Testimonials and Feedback" activity in chapter 2, write down the top five things that you learned about your business:

____

____

____

____

____

4. CRAFT A LIFELINE AND WRITE YOUR REMARKABLE BIO

Using the thoughts you gathered in the "Craft a Lifeline and Write Your Remarkable Bio" activity in chapter 2, write your remarkable bio here:

____

____

____

____

5. CREATE A GREAT TAGLINE

Using the thoughts you gathered in the "Create a Great Tagline" activity in chapter 2, write your top three taglines here:

1. ______________________________
2. ______________________________
3. ______________________________

6. IDENTIFY AND BRAND YOUR WEIRD

Using the thoughts you gathered in the "Identify and Brand Your Weird" activity in chapter 2, write your "weird" here.

7. EXTRACT YOUR PILLARS

From the "Extract Your Pillars" activity in chapter 2, write your three pillars here:

1.
2.
3.

8. IMAGINE YOUR VISUAL IDENTITY

From the "Imagine Your Visual Identity" activity in chapter 3, attach a photo of your sample mood board here.

9. CONSIDER THE BUSINESS TYPES

Using the thoughts you gathered from the "Consider the Business Types" activity in chapter 4, what are your three favorite business types and how would you use them for your business?

10. CONSIDER THE SERVICE MODELS

Using the thoughts you gathered from the "Consider the Service Models" activity in chapter 4, what are your three favorite service models and how would you use them for your business?

11. BOOK A ONE-TO-ONE SESSION

The "Book a One-to-One Session" activity in chapter 5 asked you to book and attend an in-person or online session. What did you learn from this session and how can you apply these lessons to your business?

___

___

___

12. TAKE STOCK OF YOUR ONE-TO-ONE BUSINESS

From the "Take Stock of Your One-to-One Business" activity in chapter 5, list three strategies you are already using in your one-to-one business and how:

___

___

___

Now, write down three strategies you plan to use more effectively in your one-to-one business and how:

___

___

___

13. BOOK A GROUP SESSION

The "Book a Group Session" activity in chapter 5 asked you to book and attend an in-person or online session. What did you learn from this session and how can you apply these lessons to your business?

___

___

___

___

14. JOURNAL YOUR MOST MEMORABLE SESSIONS

Using the thoughts you gathered from the "Journal Your Most Memorable Sessions" activity in chapter 5, what are your top three most memorable sessions and why? For each, note how you can apply something similar to your business.

___

___

___

15. CREATE A SAMPLE WORKSHOP, TRAINING, IMMERSION, OR RETREAT CALCULATOR

Using the thoughts you gathered from the "Create a Sample Workshop, Training, Immersion, or Retreat Calculator" activity in chapter 7, what are three adjustments you can make to increase your take-home pay?

16. TAKE YOUR OWN VIRTUAL CLASS

Using the thoughts you gathered from the "Take Your Own Virtual Class" activity in chapter 7, what are three things you learned when taking someone else's class and how can you use those things to improve your own classes?

17. TAKE A TRAINING, OR INVITE A GUEST

Using the thoughts you gathered from the "Take a Training, Or Invite a Guest" activity in chapter 7, what are three things you can improve and how?

If you invited a guest to take one of your classes, what three bits of feedback can you use to improve your classes?

18. EXAMINE YOUR PRODUCTS

Using the thoughts you gathered from the "Examine Your Products" activity in chapter 8, what are three products you can offer in the future and how?

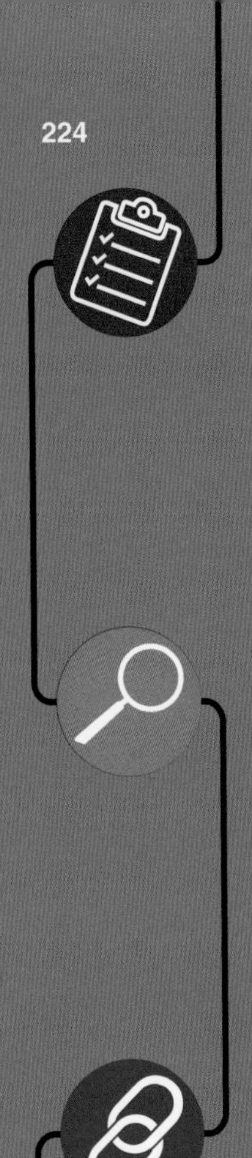

19. LIST YOUR FAVORITE PRODUCTS

Using the thoughts you gathered from the "List Your Favorite Products" activity in chapter 9, what are three products from your list that you could easily find local collaborations for? Explain how.

____

____

____

20. IDENTIFY PRODUCT AND MERCHANDISE IDEAS

Using the thoughts you gathered from the "Identify Product and Merchandise Ideas" activity in chapter 9, what are the top three ideas that you could easily incorporate into your existing service models? Explain how.

____

____

____

21. REFLECT ON YOUR CURRENT BUSINESS SERVICE MODELS

Using the thoughts you gathered from the "Reflect on Your Current Business Service Models" activity in chapter 10, what are the top three things you have learned about your current business?

____

____

____

22. REFLECT ON YOUR WEEKLY WORKFLOW

Using the thoughts you gathered from the "Reflect on Your Weekly Workflow" activity in chapter 10, what are the top three things you have learned about your workweek?

____

____

____

23. REFLECT ON YOUR CASH FLOW

Using the thoughts you gathered from the "Reflect on Your Cash Flow" activity in chapter 10, what are the top three things you have learned about your current cash flow situation?

____

____

____

24. MAXIMIZE YOUR EXISTING BUSINESS

Using the thoughts you gathered from the "Maximize Your Existing Business" activity in chapter 11, what is one way you could tighten up the costs associated with each service model? Explain how.

One-to-one sessions: ______________________________

____

Group sessions: ______________________________

____

Conferences and festivals: ______________________________

____

Workshops: ______________________________

____

Immersions: ______________________________

____

Retreats: ______________________________

____

Trainings:______________________________

____

Products and merchandise: ______________________________

____

25. SET REALISTIC AND MANAGEABLE GOALS

Using the thoughts you gathered from the "Set Realistic and Manageable Goals" activity in chapter 11, what is one realistic 24-month goal that you could achieve for each service model? Explain how.

One-to-one sessions: ______________________________

____

Group sessions: ______________________________

____

Conferences and festivals: ______________________________

____

Workshops: ______________________________

____

Immersions: ______________________________

____

Retreats: ______________________________

____

Trainings: ______________________________

____

Products and merchandise: ______________________________

____

26. ASSESS YOUR PAID CONTENT

Using the thoughts you gathered from the "Assess Your Paid Content" activity in chapter 12, what is one area of opportunity for better branding for the goods and services under each of your pillars?

Pillar 1: ______________________________

Area of opportunity: ______________________________

____

Pillar 2: ______________________________

Area of opportunity: ______________________________

____

Pillar 3: ______________________________

Area of opportunity: ______________________________

____

27. ASSESS YOUR FREE CONTENT

Using the thoughts you gathered from the "Assess Your Free Content" activity in chapter 12, what is one area of opportunity for better branding for the goods and services under each of your pillars?

Pillar 1: ______________________________

Area of opportunity: ______________________________

____

Pillar 2: ______________________________

Area of opportunity: ______________________________

____

Pillar 3: ______________________________

Area of opportunity: ______________________________

____

28. BRAINSTORM GRASSROOTS MARKETING OPPORTUNITIES

Using the thoughts you gathered from the "Brainstorm Grassroots Marketing Opportunities" activity in chapter 13, what are your top three ideal places to give out business cards? Explain how you plan to connect.

____

____

____

29. TAKE STOCK OF YOUR DIGITAL MARKETING

Using the thoughts you gathered from the "Take Stock of Your Digital Marketing" activity in chapter 14, what are the top three digital marketing elements that you use in your current business?

____

____

____

What are three digital marketing elements that you could use more frequently in your current business? Explain how.

____

____

____

30. OBSERVE EVENT MARKETING

Using the thoughts you gathered from the "Take Stock of Your Digital Marketing" activity in chapter 15, what are the top three characteristics from other businesses' event marketing that you love and can incorporate into your yoga business? Explain how.

____

____

____

31. CREATE YOUR MARKETING SCHEDULE

Using the thoughts you gathered from the "Create Your Marketing Schedule" activity in chapter 16, what goods and services do you plan to market in the next few months. How do you plan to market them?

____

____

____

____

32. WRITE YOUR ELEVATOR INTRODUCTION

From the “Write Your Elevator Introduction” activity in chapter 17, write your elevator introduction here:

33. WRITE YOUR PITCH LETTER OR DIRECT MESSAGE

From the “Write Your Pitch Letter or Direct Message” activity in chapter 17, write your final pitch letter or direct message here:

34. CREATE YOUR HOT LIST

Using the thoughts you gathered from the “Create Your Hot List” activity in chapter 17, who are the top three people on your hot list? Explain what you can do for them.

35. SET MIDPOINT GOALS

Using the thoughts you gathered from the "Set Midpoint Goals" activity in chapter 18, what is one realistic 12-month midpoint goal that you could achieve for each service model? Explain how.

One-to-one sessions: ______________________________

____

Group sessions: ______________________________

____

Conferences and festivals: ______________________________

____

Workshops: ______________________________

____

Immersions: ______________________________

____

Retreats: ______________________________

____

Trainings: ______________________________

____

Products and merchandise: ______________________________

____

36. CHOOSE BRIDGE STRATEGIES

Using the thoughts you gathered from the "Choose Bridge Strategies" activity in chapter 18, what one realistic bridge strategy that you could achieve for each service model? Explain how.

One-to-one sessions: ______________________________

____

Group sessions: ______________________________

____

Conferences and festivals: ______________________________

____

Workshops: ______________________________

____

Immersions: ____________________

____

Retreats: ____________________

____

Trainings: ____________________

____

Products and merchandise: ____________________

____

37. REVAMP YOUR WORKWEEK

Using the thoughts you gathered from the "Revamp Your Workweek" activity in chapter 19, what are three ways you can revamp your workweek to allow time to focus on the big four?

____

____

____

REFERENCES

Desikachar, T.K.V. 2011. *Health, Healing, and Beyond: Yoga and the Living Tradition of T. Krishnamacharya.* New York: North Point Press.

Elnaj, S. *The 'New Normal' And The Future Of Technology After The Covid-19 Pandemic.* Forbes Technology Council. January 25, 2021. https://www.forbes.com/sites/forbestechcouncil/2021/01/25/the-new-normal-and-the-future-of-technology-after-the-covid-19-pandemic/?sh=1166b6fb6bbb

Napoletano, E. 2012. "Rethinking Unpopular." Filmed February 29, 2012, in Boulder, Colorado. TEDx video. www.youtube.com/watch?v=S4DOJpB2I8o.

Sinek, S. 2009. "Start With Why: How Great Leaders Inspire Action." Filmed September 28, 2009, in Puget Sound, Washington. TEDx video. www.youtube.com/watch?v=u4ZoJKF_VuA.

Wilson, F. 2019. *Kilted Yoga: Yoga Laid Bare*. London: Yellow Kite.

INDEX

ABOUT THE AUTHOR

Ava Taylor is an avid yogi and a tenacious, creative entrepreneur.

As the founder of YAMA Talent, Ava optimizes yoga businesses through her ability to strategically discern the strengths and opportunities of her clients and through her understanding of each business owner's unique position in the market.

She is the go-to strategist for yoga business owners looking to get their businesses to the next level. She is known for clarifying both purpose and direction for her clients and for instilling the confidence needed to get there.

Her personal mission is to bring the tools of yoga and wellness to communities of all kinds.

Throughout her career Taylor has collaborated with over 1,000 yoga teachers, studio owners, and brands around the globe. She has transformed what was previously a mom-and-pop industry with a professional infrastructure she pioneered for booking, artist management, and consultation. This earned her a remarkable reputation for helping yoga business owners expand and succeed.

Taylor is a sought-out contributor in the media, known for having unparalleled market knowledge, access to key players, and the inside track on the latest in data and trends. She holds a degree in intercultural communication from Pepperdine University. She has held senior roles in marketing, operations, and sales as well as running her own business for well over a decade.

She has been featured in the *New York Times* and has sat on the board of advisors for the Z Living television network and the Lineage Project. As a Yoga Alliance CEU provider, Ava conducted crisis management during the COVID-19 pandemic and was the lead contributor for the EKA Business Support Services initiative with the Yoga Alliance Foundation. Taylor coproduced the annual yoga garden at the White House during the Obama administration and both of the yoga classes in Central Park with over 10,000 attendees.

Based in New York City, she travels the world doing yoga with her clients and community as often as she can.

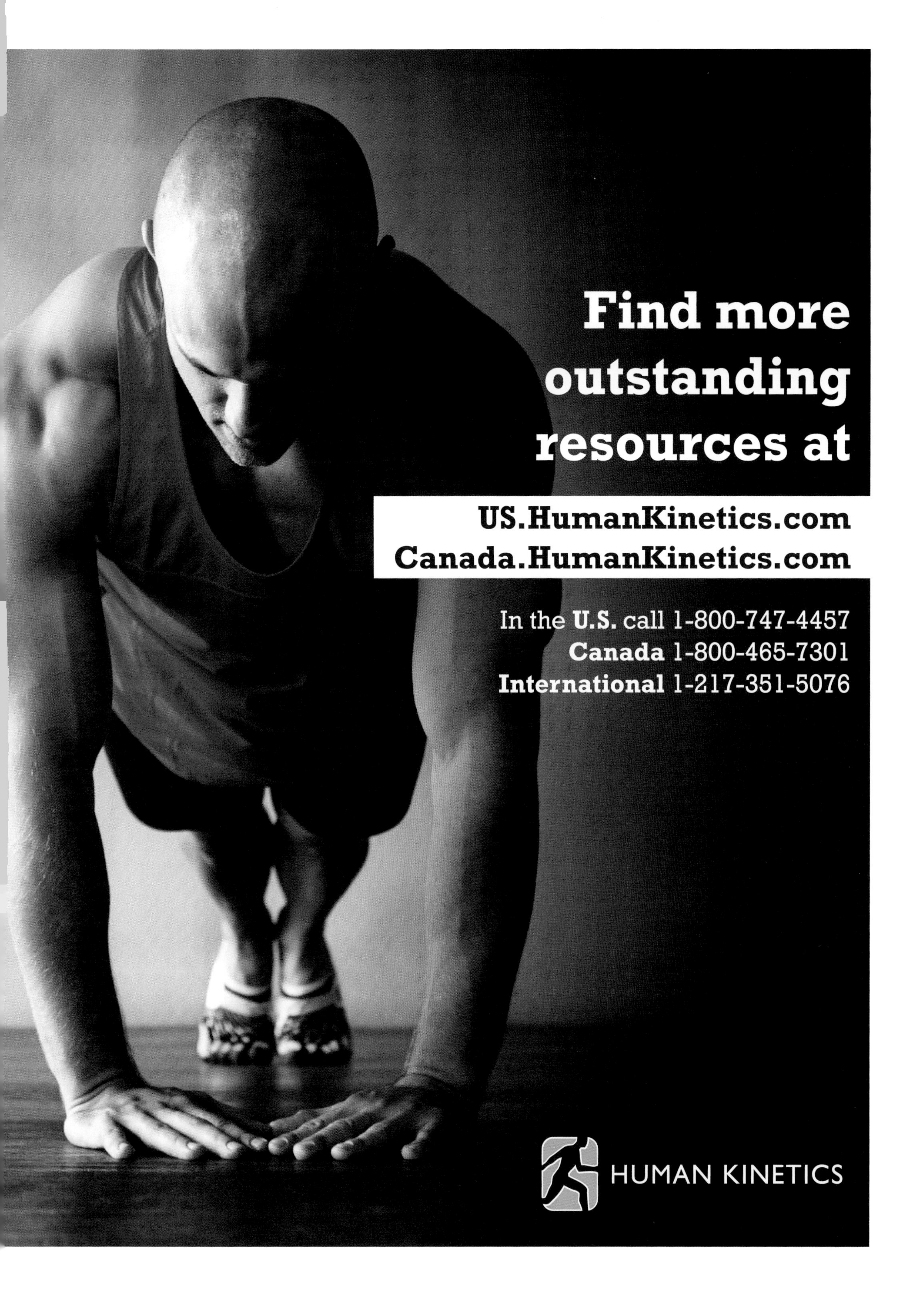

Find more outstanding resources at
US.HumanKinetics.com
Canada.HumanKinetics.com
In the U.S. call 1-800-747-4457
Canada 1-800-465-7301
International 1-217-351-5076
HUMAN KINETICS